CW00832605

My Ladys Soul: The Poems of Elizabeth Eleanor Siddall

edited with an introduction and notes
by Serena Trowbridge

Victorian Secrets 2018

Published by

Victorian Secrets Limited
32 Hanover Terrace
Brighton BN2 9SN

www.victoriansecrets.co.uk

My Ladys Soul: The Poems of Elizabeth Eleanor Siddall
This Victorian Secrets edition 2018

Introduction and notes © 2018 by Serena Trowbridge
This edition © 2018 by Victorian Secrets
Composition and design by Catherine Pope

All rights reserved. The use of any part of this publication reproduced, transmitted in any form or by any means, electronic, mechanical, photocopying, recording, or otherwise, or stored in a retrieval system, without prior consent of the publisher, constitutes an infringement of the copyright law.

A catalogue record for this book is available from the British Library.

ISBN 978-1-906469-62-7

CONTENTS

Images

1. Front cover: Anna Mary Howitt, "Elizabeth Siddall", pencil on paper, 1854 (Mark Samuels Lasner Collection, on loan to the University of Delaware Library)

2. Dante Gabriel Rossetti, "Elizabeth Siddall", pencil on paper, 1855 (Mark Samuels Lasner Collection, on loan to the University of Delaware Library), page 19

3. Barbara Leigh Smith Bodichon, "Elizabeth Siddall", pencil on paper, 1854 (Mark Samuels Lasner Collection, on loan to the University of Delaware Library), page 48

4. MS "Life and night are falling from me", Ashmolean Museum, WA1977.182 , Image © Ashmolean Museum, University of Oxford, page 56

5. Elizabeth Siddall, "The Woeful Victory", pencil, brown and black ink on paper, 1860 (Mark Samuels Lasner Collection, on loan to the University of Delaware Library), page 94

6. Elizabeth Siddall, Autograph letter to Georgiana Burne-Jones, 12 March 1861 (Mark Samuels Lasner Collection, on loan to the University of Delaware Library), page 105

This book is for Edward, who is starting to love poetry as much as I do.

INTRODUCTION

Elizabeth Siddall is known as a model for the Pre-Raphaelite Brotherhood, and increasingly as an artist, but her poetry remains generally obscure despite its appearance in some anthologies of Victorian poetry. Few people read her poetry critically, which raises questions about why is it so difficult to take her poems seriously. A great deal has been written about Siddall's life in recent years, but not since 1978 has there been an attempt to publish her poems as a collection.[1] Instead, the woman has come to be represented purely by her face. In this short book, I intend to introduce the reader to Siddall's poems, and to suggest some ways in which it might be possible to give her writing critical attention. Although there are only sixteen poems extant, plus a few fragments, there are enough to give an idea of the kind of poet she was, and to draw some wider conclusions about her work.[2]

Few female figures of the nineteenth century have engaged the popular imagination as much as Elizabeth Eleanor Siddall. For most people, their first experience of Siddall – or "Lizzie", as she tends to be popularly known – is as the wife and muse of Dante Gabriel Rossetti, and model for paintings such as John Everett Millais's *Ophelia* (1852, Tate Britain). Her face is very familiar; her rather short and sad life almost equally so, having been depicted in novels, biography, television and even poetry. Her life appears to be of more interest than her work, then; she seems to exist in our consciousness of the Victorian period as a woman who represents the repressed, neglected and 'fallen' females of the time.[3] Moreover, she is as famous for her death as her life: it is her suicide, her burial with Rossetti's poems, and

---

1 Mark Samuels Lasner and Roger C. Lewis, *Poems and Drawings of Elizabeth Siddal* (Wolfville, N.S.: Wombat Press, 1978). This was part of a limited run and is now difficult to obtain. The poems also appear in the final chapter of Marsh's *Legend*.

2 A great deal of work has been done on researching the life story of Elizabeth Siddall, so I include a timeline of her life events in this book rather than a summary biography, as well as a bibliography of works relating to Siddall for further reading.

3 For more discussion of Siddall as an 'icon' of Victorian femininity, see Jan Marsh's book *The Legend of Elizabeth Siddal* (London: Quartet Books, 1989).

the subsequent ghoulish exhumation for which she is now most famous. The myths about her abound: how she was discovered in a milliner's shop and introduced to the Pre-Raphaelite Brotherhood; her tempestuous relationship with Rossetti; the stillbirth of their child; her (probably mythical) suicide note; how her hair allegedly carried on growing after her death. Perhaps it is this legendary quality to her life, mournful and melancholic, which appeals. She seems to be the reverse of her sister-in-law, the poet Christina Rossetti, who is stereotyped as a spinster who was chaste and overly religious. Yet neither of these views is entirely true, and neither is useful. Siddall is, as Jan Marsh perceptively discussed in *The Legend of Elizabeth Siddal*, constantly mythologised, and these mythologies are reformed and reframed to suit our own needs. Marsh, among others, attempts to separate her from her myths, but it is very difficult to do so, so insistent and pervasive are the stories which shroud her vanishing figure. As Alison Chapman points out, while Siddall was "valued in the nineteenth century for her status as muse, any recovery of her art and poetry is inevitably bound up with the ideology that both produced and silenced her work".[4]

Griselda Pollock and Deborah Cherry also protest the elision of Siddall into the Pre-Raphaelite muse, arguing in "Woman as Sign" that she is a constructed figure who bolsters her husband's reputation, and is a signifier for his status and power, for "masculine creativity",[5] which is "erected on the negation of the female model".[6] Significantly, they also take issue with the variant spellings of her name as an example of how the woman was constructed as a Pre-Raphaelite icon; though few have done so since their work was published, I have chosen to follow their lead in this. Their argument is essentially that "Siddal" is a "deliberate misspelling", and that "Siddall, a historical individual" is replaced in Pre-Raphaelite literature as "Siddal" who "functions as a sign of the genius of Dante Gabriel Rossetti", is "constructed as fatally ill" and is consequently

4 Alison Chapman, *The Afterlife of Christina Rossetti* (New York: Macmillan, 2000), p. 38.

5 Griselda Pollock and Deborah Cherry, "Woman as Sign in Pre-Raphaelite Literature: The Representation of Elizabeth Siddall", in *Vision and Difference: Feminism, Femininity and Histories of Art* (London: Routledge, 2003), pp.128-162 (p. 132).

6 Pollock and Cherry, p. 132.

unable to exist outside the Pre-Raphaelite circle which made her famous.[7] Since my focus here is to suggest the value of Siddall's poetry, not as an addition to Rossetti's but in its own right, I find Pollock and Cherry's suggestion appropriate for my work.

Today those with an interest in Siddall – academic or otherwise – are more likely to see her as an iconic example of abused womanhood, a victim whose beauty transcends her life, patient and suffering as we see her in *Beata Beatrix* (1870, Tate Britain). This often leads to interesting discussions on the subject of Victorian women, but it is based on her life, and in truth we have relatively little to go on. We know the main facts of her life, but we have no diaries and few letters, and some facts remain murky despite extensive research. Furthermore, she remains an ambiguous character: we can never know the realities of her marriage, her addiction and her death, and it is possibly because of these shadowy areas that she has so much appeal: it is possible to invent what we don't know. In *Beata Beatrix*, Dante's beloved is seen in a spiritual ecstasy which prefigures her death, indicated by symbols within the painting which reference the *Vita Nuova*. Rossetti conflates the historical/fictional relationship of Dante and Beatrice with his relationship with Siddall in much of his work, constructing a modern myth of intense, enduring but doomed love. Rossetti is memorialising his dead wife, using Dante's poetry as a vehicle to express his own distress. These open-ended myths behind the painting have perhaps contributed to its appeal. As Lynne Pearce has pointed out, "the popular success of *Beata Beatrix* would seem to derive from the very fact that the figure in the painting is an 'outline' that has *not* been filled in. Based on a literary legend that the twentieth-century audience is unlikely to be conversant with, Rossetti's hazy vision of a semi-conscious woman succeeds because of its vicariousness."[8] Siddall herself becomes a vehicle in these paintings, then, for male desire and for poetic longing, which makes it difficult to see her as a creative figure in her own right.

---

7 Pollock and Cherry, pp. 131-2.

8 Lynne Pearce, *Woman Image Text: Readings in Pre-Raphaelite Art and Literature* (Hemel Hempstead: Harvester Wheatsheaf, 1991), p. 51.

Siddall as Artist

Siddall's interest in art was inspired by her experience as a model and her immersion into the world of the Pre-Raphaelite Brotherhood. As Rossetti's pupil, she learned her skill from him, but he, Ruskin and Morris were impressed with her work, and insisted on her independent skill and creativity, and there are some who still share this view, though she is often sidelined in comparison with other, more prolific, female artists of the period. There were two significant indicators of the esteem in which her work was held by her peers; the first is Ruskin's patronage of Siddall's work, in which he not only expanded her artistic and cultural horizons, funding a trip to Paris both for health and education, for example, but also arranged and paid for medical treatment. When he first saw her work, early in 1855, he "declared them to be better than Rossetti's own and promptly bought them all".[9] Ruskin's patronage was encouraging as well as financially rewarding – he paid Siddall an annuity of £150 a year in return for all the work she produced – but it was also restricting, in some ways. Nicknaming her "Ida", "the "strange Poet-princess" whose "grand/imaginations" inspire the exclusively female academy in Tennyson's *The Princess*, which "ranked her among the geniuses",[10] Ruskin's control over Siddall's life and work was excessive, and lasted only a year.

The other indicator of Siddall's growing significance as an artist was the inclusion of four of her works in a small exhibition in Russell Place, Marylebone of Pre-Raphaelite art in 1857, and then included in the British Art exhibition which toured America; a painting was bought by the Massachusetts collector Charles Eliot Norton. Siddall was the only female artist to be included in the Marylebone exhibition, and the reception was generally favourable, though as Marsh and Nunn point out, "[t]hese were the only occasions on which her work was shown publicly",[11] possibly due to ill-health.

---

9   John Dixon Hunt, *The Wider Sea: A Life of John Ruskin* (London: Phoenix, 1998), p. 248.

10   Joseph Bristow, "'Any Day that You're a Good Boy': Ruskin's Patronage, Rossetti's Expectations", *Ruskin and Gender*, ed. Dinah Birch and Francis O'Gorman (Basingstoke: Palgrave, 2002), pp. 137-58 (pp. 148-9).

11   Jan Marsh and Pamela Gerrish Nunn, *Women Artists and the Pre-Raphaelite Movement* (London: Virago, 1989), p. 71.

Siddall was evidently encouraged by the Pre-Raphaelite Brotherhood in her artistic ambitions from the early 1850s, and despite a lack of her own materials produced a number of small works which were mostly inspired by poetry, especially the ballads collected by Sir Walter Scott, whose medievalized influence is apparent in her poetry as well as her art, and whose work also influenced the ballads of Dante Gabriel Rossetti, such as "Sister Helen" and "Stratton Water". Other sources of inspiration include the Bible and Shakespeare; her works include "Jephthah's Daughter", "Lady Macbeth", "The Gay Goshawk" and "Sir Galahad and the Holy Grail". The influence of Pre-Raphaelitism is apparent in both subject and style, though at least to begin with her "figures tend to be stiff and anatomically awkward".[12] The Brotherhood were enthusiastic about her work, however, feeling it to be new and exciting in its untutoredness and originality, and there were plans for her work to provide illustrations to poems, for a collection of ballads to be edited by William Allingham, and for the Moxon Tennyson; many of these works were begun by Siddall but few completed and none published.

Several scholars have looked seriously at her art: the Ruskin Gallery, Sheffield, held an exhibition of her work in 1991, with a catalogue by Jan Marsh and 58 paintings and drawings included. Marsh, in several books, discusses Siddall's painting, pointing out that it "is remarkable that she asserted her claim to a creative role from which her gender, class and occupation tended to exclude her".[13] Marsh's work has rescued Siddall's life and painting from the shadow of Rossetti, and emphasised the genuine skill apparent in her work, dismissing those who insist that the drawings and paintings are derivative, lacking in talent, and uninteresting. There are a number of pencil sketches and studies by Siddall, as well as "small, intense watercolours",[14] and a few oils; Marsh suggests that there may be more yet to be found. Recognition of the artistic value of her work in its own right is increasing; Deborah Cherry writes that:

By the mid-1850s Siddall had developed a distinctive artistic

12 Marsh and Nunn, p. 66.

13 Jan Marsh, *Pre-Raphaelite Sisterhood* (London: Quartet, 1998), p. 35.

14 Marsh, Jan, *Elizabeth Siddal 1829-1862: Pre-Raphaelite Artist* (Sheffield: Ruskin Gallery, Collection of the Guild of St George/Sheffield Arts Department, 1991), p. 24.

style characterized by compositional layering, enclosed space, attenuated figures and jewel-like colours in which the furniture, dress and bulky folds of the drapery, as well as the execution in watercolour, consciously rework pre-modern visual languages.[15] Cherry argues that Siddall's work was not just influenced by Pre-Raphaelitism but influences it in turn, making the medieval style and setting of the paintings absolutely her own. This growing acknowledgement of Siddall's individual talent as an artist is significant, suggesting that recent criticism is permitting her to step out of the shadows of her male peers.

Siddall as Poet

There is, then, a satisfying trend towards the recognition of Siddall's art. The same cannot be said of her poetry, even during her lifetime; as Marsh points out, none of her associates and friends mention her writing, and thus we assume it must have been a private activity, though Violet Hunt suggests she had been writing from the age of 11.[16] It is not completely overlooked now: a few poems occasionally appear in anthologies of Victorian poetry;[17] and the biographies, from Hunt's shocking *The Wife of Rossetti* to Lucinda Hawksley's *Lizzie Siddal: The Tragedy of a Pre-Raphaelite Supermodel*, rely heavily on the poems as 'evidence' of her state of mind. Yet as far as I can tell, there are currently only three scholarly considerations of Siddall's poetry which examine its literary art and merit, and those are the short final chapter to Marsh's *Legend*, an excellent article by Constance Hassett, "Elizabeth Siddal's Poetry: A Problem and Some Suggestions", which appeared in *Victorian Poetry* in 1997, and a chapter, "Sleep and Liberation: the Opiate World of Elizabeth Siddal", in Béatrice Laurent, *Sleeping Beauties in Victorian Britain: Cultural, Literary and Ar-*

---

15 Deborah Cherry, "Elizabeth Eleanor Siddall", in Elizabeth Prettejohn (ed.), *The Cambridge Companion to the Pre-Raphaelites* (Cambridge: CUP, 2012), pp. 183-195 (p. 183).

16 Marsh, *Elizabeth Siddal, Pre-Raphaelite Artist*, p. 30.

17 "A Silent Wood" and "Dead Love" appear in *The New Oxford Book of Victorian Verse*, ed. Christopher Ricks (Oxford: OUP, 1990); "The Lust of the Eyes", "Worn Out", "At Last" and "Love and Hate" are included in *The Broadview Anthology of Victorian Poetry and Poetic Theory*, ed. Thomas J. Collins and Vivienne J. Rundle (Plymouth: Broadview Press, 2005).

tistic Explorations of a Myth, though this also focuses on Siddall's life and art. All three of these assert the quality of Siddall's poetry, with Hassett noting that she was "a poet of some skill and poignancy",[18] while Arcara notes the tendency to read her works as biographical, the miserable musings of a depressed woman with poetical tendencies rather than talent. A specific approach is taken to one poem in Sandra M. Donaldson's article "'Ophelia' in Elizabeth Siddal Rossetti's Poem 'A Year and a Day'", while a broader and generally laudatory approach is taken by Maggie Berg in her review of Lewis and Lasner's edition, "A Neglected Voice: Elizabeth Siddal". Berg asserts that Siddall's work is "certainly superior to other peripheral Pre-Raphaelites",[19] though with a focus on the personal nature of the poems.

Perhaps as a consequence of this view, the poems do not seem to have gained credibility in critical works on nineteenth-century literature. Partly this is due to Siddall's mythologised, idealised status, which one needs to reject to explore her work fully. Another problem with writing on Siddall's poetry, as Hassett comments, is that given her extant work stands at sixteen poems plus a few fragments, we cannot use the standard critical terms for any analysis: it is not possible to look at development over time, to recognise many recurrent features, or to see any trajectory in her work. Moreover, we do not know the dates of composition for most of the poems, and even the titles were mostly added posthumously. Yet in an age when there is great enthusiasm for reclaiming the work of 'forgotten' writers, however large or small, fragmentary or dispersed their output was, it is surprising that more attention has not been paid to Siddall, and I hope that this edition may encourage others to consider her work in more detail.

It is worth noting that although her poems tend towards melancholy, and display a frequently negative view of romantic relationships, this is not uncommon for the period, as Hassett and Arcara have pointed out; and indeed there are many parallels between Siddall's work and her sister-in-law, Christina Rossetti's. Siddall's poems in particular have a strong tendency towards medieval imagery, which is also evident in her draw-

---

18 Constance Hassett, "Elizabeth Siddal's Poetry: A Problem and Some Suggestions", *Victorian Poetry*, 1997, 35.4, 443-470 (p. 443)

19 Maggie Berg, "A Neglected Voice: Elizabeth Siddal [Review article]", *Dalhousie Review* (1980), 151-56 (p. 151)

ings, and it is possible that some of these poems were intended to accompany her artwork. Despite the medievalism of the aesthetics in the poems, though, it is interesting to note that the language used is uniformly contemporary: there are no archaisms in the poems apart from "Ope not thy lips" and "Christ ye save yon bonny shepherd", though this latter sounds like an imitation of rustic speech rather than archaic language. There are few strained rhymes, unexpected contractions or other self-consciously historic uses of language such as other poets of the period sometimes display, which gives the poems an attractive straightforwardness. Their form also tends to be deceptively simple, but there is undoubted skill in the crafting of the poems despite their status as drafts. Significantly, "although her themes are common to the entire Pre-Raphaelite movement, they become unique because of the strength of the female voice."[20] That voice clearly comes from a different situation than that of the other notable female Pre-Raphaelite poet, Christina Rossetti, who writes with a more identifiably Christian voice and from a position, relatively speaking, of confidence in her own voice which falters sometimes in Siddall's work. Siddall, though, writes as a woman who knows what it is to be valued only for her appearance, as a woman who has to fight to be taken seriously.

Siddall is a poet who engages with the natural world in complex ways throughout her work. As Sandra Donaldson points out, the speaker in many of the poems, especially "It is not now a longing year", "interacts with the world outside the self, and, in facing nature, she faces her own nature".[21] Her repeated references to "green leaves" and the beauty of nature is often undermined by its failure to bring comfort. Many of the poems have colder imagery: "Life and night are falling from me" and "Many a mile over land and sea" present a frozen landscape in which nature's chilly beauty reflects the attitude of the speaker without providing a hospitable setting for suffering.

20   Rhonda Brock-Servais, "Elizabeth Eleanor Siddal" in *Nineteenth-Century British Women Writers: A Bio-Bibliographical Critical Sourcebook* ed. Abigail Burnham Bloom (Westport, CT: Greenwood Press, 2000), pp. 363-66 (p. 364).

21   Sandra M. Donaldson, "'Ophelia' in Elizabeth Siddal Rossetti's Poem 'A Year and a Day'", *Journal of Pre-Raphaelite Studies* 2 (November 1981), 127-33 (p. 128).

Poetic Influences

Cherry points out that "Siddall was an avid reader", of Romantic poetry and Border ballads as well as the poetry of her contemporaries.[22] There is an apocryphal story of how Siddall first encountered Tennyson's work on a scrap of newspaper, and her art demonstrates her engagement with the ballads collected by Scott, as well as the poetry of Keats and other Romantic poets; through her relationship with Dante Gabriel Rossetti she would have had access to a wide range of books, which we know she read with enthusiasm. Hassett makes clear the influence of the ballads upon Siddall's poems, not only in subject matter but in their simple, almost naïve tone and lexical choices, though with relatively few archaisms. Her frequent use of quatrains similarly points to the influence of ballads, as well as her subjects of female loss and longing in some poems.

Much has been made of Siddall's potentially difficult relationship with Christina Rossetti, assuming the disapproval of her religious sister-in-law, but there is little evidence for this. However, their relationship may have been strongly inflected with poetry, since there are some remarkable parallels between the two poets' work, and Christina Rossetti would have provided Siddall with her only close female poetic role model. Frequently, Christina Rossetti's poem "In an Artist's Studio" is cited to "explain" Siddall and her relationship with Dante Gabriel Rossetti, demonstrating a sympathy for the situation of the artist's model, but it is rare that Siddall is allowed to speak for herself, though she does this clearly in poems such as "I care not for my Ladys soul". Christina Rossetti's poems manifest the influence of Pre-Raphaelitism, though as Chapman notes, she "does not simply reiterate the representational registers of the Pre-Raphaelite aesthetic",[23] but inverts, enhances and explores them. Siddall, likewise, demonstrates a Pre-Raphaelite interest in colour, shape and form, as well as a simple medievalized style, but like Christina Rossetti she presents these from a woman's perspective; many of the poems offer the sadness of loss, but with an awareness of the fickleness of masculine love for the muse or model; some use bitterness, while others suggest passive acceptance. The hopelessness of female life is tempered in both poets' work by

---

22 Cherry, "Elizabeth Eleanor Siddall", p. 184.

23 Alison Chapman, *The Afterlife of Christina Rossetti* (New York: Macmillan, 2000), p. 102.

the beauty of the world around them and the consolations of art, however flimsy and temporal those may be.

Siddall's poems offer a woman's voice, then, in situations where a woman might more usually be silent in Victorian poetry. Those who consider her work too close to Dante Gabriel Rossetti's might reflect on Swinburne's comment:

> There is the same note of originality in discipleship which distinguishes her work in art – Gabriel's influence and example not more perceptible than her own independence and freshness of inspiration.[24]

The dead or dying woman, the deserted or bereaved woman, the muse, is speaking in her work, voiced in a way Dante Gabriel Rossetti's muses are not. The female figure in Victorian art and poetry is often an aestheticized corpse, a beautiful, silenced woman; Antony H. Harrison points out that this is particularly the case in Dante Gabriel Rossetti's work.[25] As Anna Jamison suggests, however, in Christina Rossetti's work, and I would argue also in Siddall's, this woman has a voice.[26] Siddall's women speak in a voice of less restraint than Christina Rossetti's, but similarly their exterior is absent; these women may inhabit gloves or wear jewels, they may be desired for their "star-like" eyes, but they exist in their minds rather than their bodies; their physical aspect is "gone", as one poem suggests.

At the beginning of this introduction, I asked why we find it so difficult to take Siddall's poetry seriously. As I suggested, in many ways this is due to the extent to which the woman and her work have been subsumed in dusty clouds of Pre-Raphaelite myth. The answer, I think, lies in firstly examining her poems *as* poems, not as biographical manifestations from a Pre-Raphaelite idol. We need to look at them as though we have no idea where they came from – which is often difficult. And we also need to look at them in their wider context: in the context of Victorian poetic conventions, and other poetry of the time, particularly that by other women,

24 A. Swinburne, *The Swinburne Letters*, ed. Cecil Lang (New Haven: Yale University Press, 1962), vol. VI, p. 94.

25 Antony H. Harrison, *Christina Rossetti in Context* (Brighton: Harvester, 1988), p. 94.

26 Anna Jamison, "Passing Strange: Christina Rossetti's Unusual Dead", *Textual Practice*, 20.2 (2006), 257-80.

such as Adelaide Proctor, Agnes Robinson and Dora Greenwell as well as Christina Rossetti and the Brontës – though her poetry does not always demonstrate the critical sophistication of some of these poets. Nonetheless, such consideration demonstrates Siddall's interest in contemporary forms and ideas, as well as her often dramatic and appealing simplicity. Such methods of reading offer a new way of looking at Elizabeth Siddall as a poet.

William Michael Rossetti as Editor

It seems likely that modern perceptions of Siddall's life and work are at least in part due to the way in which her reception has been coloured by William Michael Rossetti. As the self-appointed guardian of his family's reputation, both literary and moral, he took it upon himself both to promote and obscure Dante Gabriel Rossetti, Christina Rossetti and Siddall. In the case of Christina Rossetti, he damaged popular views of her work in some ways, by tending towards biographical readings of her poems whilst at the same time evading any biographical links in poems he felt were too extreme or personal. He suggests in his "Memoir" of his sister that she was a poet who wrote spontaneously, with, the implication is, little thought or skill, an assertion both damaging and untrue. William Michael Rossetti also edited his sister's poems in some cases, explaining in one case that his excisions "omitt[ed] those passages which appear to me to be either in themselves inferior, or adapted rather for spinning out the theme than intensifying it".[27] In the case of Siddall, the previously published versions are poems created by William Michael Rossetti from the fragments available to him; her early reputation rested on these and on comments published by William Michael Rossetti, including one in the Burlington Magazine in 1903. In this article, he begins with rather grudging comments:

> Her life was short, and her performances restricted in both quantity and development; but they were far from undeserving of notice, even apart from that relation which she bore to Dante Rossetti...[28]

---

27 William Michael Rossetti, *The Poetical Works of Christina Georgina Rossetti, with Memoir and Notes* (London: Macmillan, 1904), p. 382.

28 William Michael Rossetti, "Dante Rossetti and Elizabeth Siddal", *The Bur-*

The article is mostly factual, even when pertaining to Siddall's art, with little discussion or personal opinion; he is at his most appreciative when talking of her beauty or her virtue. Towards the end he comments that he had previously published some of her "scanty" poems, and acknowledges little poetic skill in her work. This approach towards her life and work has flavoured subsequent popular and critical readings of Siddall.

Publication history

None of Siddall's poems were published during her lifetime, and most only exist in a draft form, often difficult to read. Dante Gabriel Rossetti wanted to include six of Siddall's poems in Christina Rossetti's 1866 book *The Prince's Progress*, including "Oh never weep for love that is dead", but Christina's response was appreciative but uncertain: "she wrote, 'How full of beauty they are, but how painful!' She thought them 'almost too hopelessly sad for publication *en masse*'".[29] These comments also reinforce a biographical reading, with the unspoken implication that to publish them would be to expose the personal griefs of their sister-in-law. The poems were not published until the turn of the century, in various collection and reminiscences of Pre-Raphaelitism by W. M. Rossetti, and, as Griselda Pollock points out, "the major primary sources used in Pre-Raphaelite scholarship ... especially those edited by ... William Michael Rossetti – were deeply implicated in nineteenth-century ideologies of class and gender, of the artist and romance".[30] W. M. Rossetti published his edited versions of the poems, then, along with his insights into his sister-in-law's character; eight appeared in *Ruskin, Rossetti, Pre-Raphaelitism* (1899), five in *Some Reminiscences* (1906), one in the *Burlington Magazine* (1903) and one in *Dante Gabriel Rossetti. His Family-Letters with a Memoir* (1895).

"Autumnal leaves are falling" was first published in the hitherto only collected edition of Siddall's poems, *Poems and Drawings of Elizabeth*

lington *Magazine for Connoisseurs*, 1903, 1.3, 273-295 (p. 273).

29 William Michael Rossetti, "Dante Rossetti and Elizabeth Siddal", *The Burlington Magazine for Connoisseurs*, 1903, 1.3, 273-295 (p. 292).

30 Pollock and Cherry, p. 92.

Siddal by Roger Lewis and Mark Samuels Lasner (1978), a book which provides the fullest text of the poems based on the Bryson MSS. Lewis and Lasner provide an edition which resists the interpretation and tidying-up of William Michael Rossetti's editing, and what they provide is a more coherent and readable text than I offer here. The poems also appear in Jan Marsh's *Elizabeth Siddal 1829-1862: Pre-Raphaelite Artist* (1991). A few have been collected in anthologies of Victorian poetry, and all except "Autumnal leaves are falling" appear in *The Pre-Raphaelites from Rossetti to Ruskin* (Dinah Roe, 2010). Of course the poems appear, sometimes in differing forms, on a number of websites. The six incomplete fragments I include have not been published before, due no doubt to their near-illegibility and fragmentary form.

Image 2: Dante Gabriel Rossetti, 1828-1882, Elizabeth Siddall, pencil on paper, 1855 (Mark Samuels Lasner Collection, on loan to the University of Delaware Library)

TIMELINE OF EVENTS IN ELIZABETH SIDDALL'S LIFE

July 25 1829	Birth of Elizabeth Eleanor Siddall, Hatton Gardens, London
1831	The Siddall family move to Southwark
1848	The Pre-Raphaelite Brotherhood is formed towards the end of this year
1849	Siddall is discovered by Walter Deverell while she is working in a milliners' shop in Cranbourne Alley. He introduces her to members of the Pre-Raphaelite Brotherhood in the same year
1849-50	Siddall sits to Deverell as Viola for his Shakespearean painting *Twelfth Night*. In 1850 she also sits to William Holman Hunt for a girl in *A Converted British Family*
1851	She sits to Hunt again, this time as Sylvia in *The Two Gentlemen of Verona*, and models for Dante Gabriel Rossetti for the first time
1852	Siddall poses for Millais's painting *Ophelia*. She also models for Hunt and Rossetti; subsequently she sat only for Rossetti. In this year, her brother Charles dies, and she gives up her work at the milliners, becoming Rossetti's pupil as she begins her own drawing and painting
March 1854	Rossetti introduces Siddall to his sister Christina. It is acknowledged by this stage that Rossetti and Siddall have "an understanding", that is, that they were likely to marry. In this year Deverell dies, and Siddall is encouraged to visit a doctor for her poor health

1855	John Ruskin begins a patronage of Siddall to encourage her work, paying her £150 a year in return for paintings and drawings. This lasted only for two years. In this year Siddall travelled to Hastings, Somerset and France, in the hope that a different climate would improve her health
November 1856	Rossetti announces his intention to marry Siddall, but reneges, and she and her sister Clara visit Bath, where Siddall and Rossetti are later reunited
1857	Siddall is the only woman whose work is included in a private exhibition of Pre-Raphaelite paintings held in Marylebone. One of her paintings, *Clerk Saunders*, is sold to an American collector. In 1857-8 she also visits Derbyshire, and attended the Sheffield School of Art for a period, possibly staying with relatives
23 May 1860	Siddall and Rossetti marry at St Clements Church, Hastings, after a period of serious illness for Siddall. They visit France for their honeymoon
1861	Siddall suffered a stillbirth on May 2nd, and a miscarriage later that year
February 11th 1862	After an overdose of laudanum, Siddall dies at home in Chatham Place, London
1864 onwards	Rossetti begins his most famous painting of Siddall, *Beata Beatrix*, memorialising her as Beatrice to his Dante
October 1869	Siddall's grave, in which the grieving Rossetti placed his manuscript poems, is opened up to retrieve the works for publication.
1895-1903	William Michael Rossetti publishes some of Siddall's poems in memoirs of Dante Gabriel Rossetti and Pre-Raphaelitism

BIBLIOGRAPHY

Works on or relating to Siddall

There are many works on Pre-Raphaelitism which mention Siddall; those listed here have a strong focus on Siddall and her poetry, or have significant views on her work.

Arcara, Stefania, "Sleep and Liberation: the Opiate World of Elizabeth Siddal", in Béatrice Laurent (ed.), *Sleeping Beauties in Victorian Britain: Cultural, Literary and Artistic Explorations of a Myth* (Bern: Peter Lang, 2014), pp. 95-120

Bailey, Conny, "Musings on a Muse: an Appraisal of the Artist Elizabeth Eleanor Siddal", *The Review of the Pre-Raphaelite Society*, 2005, 13.2, 20-29

Berg, Maggie, "A Neglected Voice: Elizabeth Siddal [Review article]", *Dalhousie Review* (1980), 151-56

Bradley, Laurel, "Elizabeth Siddal: Drawn into the Pre-Raphaelite Circle", *Art Institute of Chicago Museum Studies*, 1992, 18.2, 136-45 + 187

Bristow, Joseph, "'Any Day that You're a Good Boy': Ruskin's Patronage, Rossetti's Expectations", in *Ruskin and Gender*, ed. Dinah Birch and Francis O'Gorman (Basingstoke: Palgrave, 2002), pp. 137-158

Brock-Servais, Rhonda, "Elizabeth Eleanor Siddal" in *Nineteenth-Century British Women Writers: A Bio-Bibliographical Critical Sourcebook* ed. Abigail Burnham Bloom (Westport, CT: Greenwood Press, 2000), pp. 363-66

Donaldson, Sandra M., "'Ophelia' in Elizabeth Siddal Rossetti's Poem 'A Year and a Day'", *Journal of Pre-Raphaelite Studies* 2 (November 1981), 127-33

Dunstan, A., "The Myth of Dante Gabriel Rossetti's 'Beata Beatrix' as Memorial Painting", *The British Art Journal*, 2010, 11.1, 89-92

Edwards, Marion R., "Elizabeth Eleanor Siddal – The Age Problem", *The Burlington Magazine*, 1977, 119.887, 110-12

Ehnenn, J.R., "'Strong Traivelling': Re-visions of Women's Subjectivity and Female Labor in the Ballad-work of Elizabeth Siddal", *Victorian Poetry* 52.2 (2014), 251-76

Hassett, Constance, "Elizabeth Siddal's Poetry: A Problem and Some Suggestions", *Victorian Poetry*, 1997, 35.4, 443-470

Hawksley, Lucinda, *Lizzie Siddal: the Tragedy of a Pre-Raphaelite Supermodel* (London : André Deutsch, 2004)

Hunt, Violet, *The Wife of Rossetti Her Life and Death, etc* (London: John Lane, 1932)

Lewis, Roger C. and Mark Samuels Lasner, *Poems and Drawings of Elizabeth Siddal* (Wolfville, N.S.: Wombat Press, 1978)

Marsh, Jan, *Elizabeth Siddal 1829-1862: Pre-Raphaelite Artist* (Sheffield : Ruskin Gallery, Collection of the Guild of St George/Sheffield Arts Department, 1991)

Marsh, Jan, *Pre-Raphaelite Sisterhood* (London: Quartet, 1998)

Marsh, Jan, *Pre-Raphaelite Women* (London: Weidenfeld & Nicolson, 1987)

Marsh, Jan, *The Legend of Elizabeth Siddal* (London: Quartet Books, 1989)

Marsh, Jan and Pamela Gerrish Nunn, *Women Artists and the Pre-Raphaelite Movement* (London: Virago 1989)

Mazzeno, Laurence W., ed., *Twenty-first Century Perspectives on Victorian Literature* (Plymouth: Rowman & Littlefield, 2014)

Mégroz, Rodolphe Louis, *Dante Gabriel Rossetti: Painter Poet of Heaven in Earth* (New York: Haskell House, 1971)

Moyle, Franny, *Desperate Romantics: The Private Lives of the Pre-Raphaelites* (London: John Murray, 2009)

Orlando, Emily, "'That I May not Faint, or Die, or Swoon': Reviving Pre-Raphaelite Women", *Women's Studies*, 2009, 38.6, 611-46

Paxton, Amanda, "Love, Dismemberment and Elizabeth Siddal's Corpus", *JPRS* 2014, 22

Pearce, Lynne, *Woman Image Text: Readings in Pre-Raphaelite Art and Literature* (Hemel Hempstead: Harvester Wheatsheaf, 1991)

Pollock, Griselda and Deborah Cherry, *Vision and Difference: Feminism, Femininity and Histories of Art* (London: Routledge, 2003)

Prettejohn, Elizabeth (ed.), *The Cambridge Companion to the Pre-Raphaelites* (Cambridge: CUP, 2012)

Prose, Francine, *The Lives of the Muses: Nine Women and the Artists they Inspired* (London: Aurum Press, 2002) "Elizabeth Siddal", pp. 99-136

Ridd, Jenny, *A Destiny Defined: Dante Gabriel Rossetti and Elizabeth Siddal in Hastings* (Edgerton Publishing, 2008)

Rossetti, William Michael, "Dante Rossetti and Elizabeth Siddal", *The Burlington Magazine for Connoisseurs*, 1903, 1.3, 273-295

Rossetti, William Michael (ed.), *Dante Gabriel Rossetti. His Family-Letters with a Memoir*, 2 vols (London: Ellis & Elvey, 1895)

Rossetti, William Michael (ed.), *Ruskin, Rossetti, Pre-Raphaelitism* (London: Allen, 1899)

Rossetti, William Michael (ed.), *Some Reminiscences*, 2 vols (New York: Scribner, 1906)

Shefer, Elaine, "Deverell, Rossetti, Siddal, and 'The Bird in the Cage'", *Art Bulletin*, 1985, 67.3, 437-48

Shefer, Elaine, "Elizabeth Siddal's 'The Lady of Shalott'", *Woman's Art Journal*, 9.1, 1988, 21-29

Starzyk, L. J., "Elizabeth Siddal and the 'Soulless Self-Reflections of Man's Skill'", *Journal of Pre-Raphaelite Studies*, 2007, 16, 8-25

Surtees, Virginia, *Rossetti's Portraits of Elizabeth Siddal: a Catalogue of the Drawings and Watercolours* (Aldershot: Scolar in association with Ashmolean Museum, Oxford, 1991)

Taylor, Beverley, "Beatrix/Creatrix: Elizabeth Siddal as Muse and Creator", *Journal of Pre-Raphaelite Studies*, 1995, 4, 29-49

Taylor, Helen Nina, "'Too individual an artist to be a mere echo': Female Pre-Raphaelite Artists as Independent Professionals", *The British Art Journal*, 2011-12, 12.3, 52-59

Tondeur, L., "Elizabeth Siddal's Hair: A Methodology for Queer Reading", *Women: a Cultural Review*, 2011, 22.4, 370-386

Uphaus, Adele, "Elizabeth Siddal: Creator and Created", *The Review of the Pre-Raphaelite Society*, 2008, 16.1, 30-43

Vitale, Zaira, "Eleonora Siddal Rossetti", *Emporium* 19 (1904), 430–47

Weintraub, Stanley, *Four Rossettis* (London: W H Lane, 1978)

Other Texts Referenced

Alexander, Marc, *A Companion to the Folklore, Myths & Customs of Britain* (Bath: BCA/Sutton Publishing, 2002)

Armstrong, Isobel, Joseph Bristow and Cath Sharrock (eds), *Nineteenth Century Women Poets* (Oxford: Clarendon Press, 1998)

Bevis, Matthew (ed.), *The Oxford Handbook of Victorian Poetry* (Oxford: Oxford University Press, 2013)

Chapman, Alison, *The Afterlife of Christina Rossetti* (New York: Macmillan, 2000)

Collins, Thomas J. and Vivienne J. Rundle, *The Broadview Anthology of Victorian Poetry and Poetic Theory*, (Plymouth: Broadview Press, 2005)

Dante Alighieri, *The Commedia and Canzoniere of Dante Alighieri,* trans. and ed. E. H. Plumptre, 2 vols (London: Isbister, 1887)

Hunt, John Dixon, *The Wider Sea: A Life of John Ruskin* (London: Phoenix, 1998)

Frazer, J.G., *The Golden Bough: A Study in Magic and Religion* (London: MacMillan, 1987)

Hole, C., *English Folklore* (London: Batsford, 1940)

Homans, Margaret, *Women Writers and Poetic Identity: Dorothy Wordsworth, Emily Brontë and Emily Dickinson* (Surrey: Princeton University Press, 1980)

Jamison, Anna, "Passing Strange: Christina Rossetti's Unusual Dead", *Textual Practice*, 20.2 (2006), 257-80

Jamieson, Robert, ed., *Popular Ballads and Songs, from Tradition, Manuscripts, and Scarce Editions* (Edinburgh: John Murray, 1806) 2 vols

Leighton, Angela and Margaret Reynolds (eds), *Victorian Women Poets: An Anthology* (Oxford: Blackwell, 1995)

Morris, William, *Poems by the Way* (London: Reeves and Turner, 1891)

Poe, Edgar Allan, *The Fall of the House of Usher and Other Writings*, ed. David Galloway (London: Penguin, 2003)

Ricks, Christopher (ed.), *The New Oxford Book of Victorian Verse*, (Oxford: OUP, 1990)

Roe, Dinah (ed.), *The Pre-Raphaelites from Rossetti to Ruskin* (London: Penguin, 2010)

Rossetti, Christina, *Christina Rossetti: The Complete Poems*, ed. Rebecca W. Crump (London: Penguin, 2005)

Rossetti, Dante Gabriel, *Collected Poetry and Prose of D. G. Rossetti*, ed. Jerome McGann (New Haven: Yale University Press, 2003)

Rossetti, William Michael, *The Poetical Works of Christina Georgina Rossetti, with Memoir and Notes* (London: Macmillan, 1904)

Rossetti, William Michael, *Rossetti Papers 1862–1870* (New York: Charles Scribner, 1903)

Swinburne, Algernon, *The Swinburne Letters*, ed. Cecil Lang (New Haven: Yale University Press, 1962), 6 vols.

Wortley-Montagu, Emmeline, *The Knight and the Enchantress* (London: Longman, 1835)

Selected Fiction Relating to Siddall's Life

Allnutt, Gillian, *Lizzie Siddall: Her Journal (1862)* (Warwick: Greville Press, 1986)

Batchelor, Paula, *Angel with Bright Hair* (London: Methuen, 1957)

Green, Jeremy, *Lizzie Siddal* (London: Bloomsbury, 2016)

Kitchen, Paddy, *The Golden Veil: a novel based on the life of Elizabeth Siddall* (London: Hamish Hamilton, 1981)

Morrissey, Kim, *Clever as Paint: The Rossettis in Love* (Toronto: Playwrights Canada Press, 2000)

Puelles, Vicente Muñoz, *Los Amantes de la Niebla* (Barcelona: Planeta, 2002)

Saizarbitoria, Ramon, *Rossetti's Obsession* (Reno: Center for Basque Studies, University of Nevada, 2006)

Savage, Elizabeth, *Willowwood: A Novel of Dante Gabriel Rossetti and Elizabeth Siddal* (Boston: G.K. Hall, 1979)

Shute, Nerina, *Victorian Love Story: A Study of the Victorian Romantics based on the life of Dante Gabriel Rossetti* (London: Jarrolds, 1954)

For discussion of fictional representations of Dante Gabriel Rossetti and Elizabeth Siddall, see Lisa Dallape Matson, *Re-Presentations of Dante Gabriel Rossetti: Portrayals in Fiction, Drama, Music and Film* (New York: Cambria Press, 2010).

NOTE ON THE TEXT

The texts of Siddall's poems are taken from the Ashmolean Museum's collection of Siddall's manuscripts, which form part of the Bryson bequest. The manuscripts are scrappy, often on torn pieces of paper, and seem to have been written hurriedly; her writing is clearer in some than in others. I have included a word only where I am fairly certain it is correct; some have question marks beside them while others have been omitted if they are illegible. This may seem disruptive to the reading experience but it is my intention to present as authentic a text as possible. Siddall's punctuation is minimal, something which William Michael Rossetti altered considerably in the case of some of the poems, and her spelling sometimes erratic. I have reproduced this and other apparent errors, since they offer a flavour of the poet's natural voice. The publication history of the poems is covered in the Introduction. The poems are provided in alphabetical order since dates are unknown in almost all cases, and the titles which William Michael Rossetti added have been replaced by the first line of the poem, except for "True Love" which Siddall titled herself.

List of Abbreviations used

CGR	Christina Georgina Rossetti
DGR	Dante Gabriel Rossetti
EES	Elizabeth Eleanor Siddall
FLM	*Dante Gabriel Rossetti. His Family-Letters with a Memoir*, 2 vols (London: Ellis & Elvey, 1895), ed. William Michael Rossetti
RRP	*Ruskin, Rossetti, Pre-Raphaelitism* (London: Allen, 1899), ed. William Michael Rossetti
SR	*Some Reminiscences*, 2 vols (New York: Scribner, 1906), ed. William Michael Rossetti
WMR	William Michael Rossetti
WR	*The Wife of Rossetti*, Violet Hunt (London: John Lane, 1932)

ACKNOWLEDGEMENTS

I'm very grateful to Mark Samuels Lasner, for his encouragement and also for allowing me use of some of the images in this book. Caroline Palmer at the Ashmolean has also been extremely helpful, poring over difficult handwriting with me on several occasions. Many of my friends have made helpful suggestions concerning the indecipherable parts of the texts, and I appreciate their patience.

Any work on Elizabeth Siddall owes a debt of gratitude to Jan Marsh for her work on recovering Siddall's life and work; a list of relevant works is included in the bibliography.

I am grateful, as ever, to my lovely colleagues at Birmingham City University, to the members of the Pre-Raphaelite Society, and to the supportive community of Pre-Raphaelite Sisters, especially Sarah Doyle, Madeleine Pearce, Stephanie Graham Piña, Dinah Roe and Kirsty Walker. Without the encouragement of these people and my family I would never have completed this book.

ABOUT THE EDITOR

Dr. Serena Trowbridge is Senior Lecturer in English Literature at Birmingham City University. Her monograph, *Christina Rossetti's Gothic* (Bloomsbury), was published in 2013, and other publications include 'Past, present, and future death in the graveyard' in *Gothic and Death* , ed. Carol Davison (Manchester University Press, 2017), '"Truth to Nature": The Pleasures and Dangers of the Environment in Christina Rossetti's Poetry' in *Victorians and the Environment*, ed. Lawrence Mazzeno (Ashgate, 2017), *Insanity and the Lunatic Asylum* (edited with Thomas Knowles), (Pickering & Chatto, 2014) and *Pre-Raphaelite Masculinities* (edited with Amelia Yeates), (Ashgate, 2014). Serena was editor of the *Review* of the Pre-Raphaelite Society 2005-2017.

My Ladys Soul

Autumnal leaves are falling

Autumnal leaves are falling
about her new made grave
Where the tall grass bends to listen
To the murmur of the wave.

Notes

Line 1: A popular concept for the passing of time; for Emily Brontë, for example, "Every leaf speaks bliss to me/Fluttering from the autumn tree" ("Autumn Leaves"). All published versions of this stanza have amended it to "Autumn leaves".

Lines 2-3: The grass which grows around the grave recalls CGR's "song (When I am dead, my Dearest)": "Be the green grass above me/ With showers and dewdrops wet;" (ll. 5-6). It also recalls Siddall's "It is not now a longing year": "I lie among the tall green grass/ That bends above my head" (ll. 19-20).

This fragment is reminiscent of other poems by Siddall, echoing not only the "tall grass" of "It is not now a longing year" but also the mourning for the dead in "True Love" and "O mother open the window wide". The quatrain deploys Siddall's familiar trope of depicting a scene in which nature is sympathetic to human life and death, here with the leaves dropping like tears while the grass swaddles the grave. The stanza above appears in Lasner's edition with a second quatrain:

Laden autumn, here I stand
With my sheaves in either hand;
Speak the word that sets me free,
Naught but rest seems good to me.

Lasner notes that: "The first quatrain has never been printed; it appears in a Bryson MS. The second quatrain was first printed by Violet Hunt in *The Wife of Rossetti: Her Life and Death* (1932), p. 283; we have found no MS. authority for it. However, in attributing these lines to EE[S] in his *Four Rossettis* (1977), Professor Stanley Weintraub was confident, he told us, that they were so characteristic of her other verse that he could chance trusting Miss Hunt."[1] Weintraub comments in *Four Rossettis* that this "fragment attributed to her was particularly foreboding, in its seeming pun on the drug she relied upon to blot out her misery",[2] and critical commentary on the poem often refers to this apparent coded reference to laudanum. Weintraub's book presents readings of a number of poems by DGR, CGR and EES, all of which rely on biography as source material.

These stanzas, if they were both by Siddall, are not likely to form one poem since there is no MS source for the second, though they are frequently published as such, particularly in online sources. The form of "Autumnal leaves" is different, in rhyme scheme and metre, to "Laden Autumn", and it is probably only the subject matter that has caused editors to link the two stanzas. On the MS, "Autumnal leaves" precedes the poem "Ruthless hands have torn her", written in the same ink, and it is possible it may be a stanza of this poem; its rhyme scheme and metre are less regular than this longer poem, but bear some similarity, and it is possible that further work was intended on this particular stanza.

The stanza "Laden Autumn" is, however, more likely to be the work of William Morris, since a version of it appears in his *Poems by the Way* under "Verses for Pictures",[3] along with stanzas for the other three seasons, with which it makes a convincing set. The difference in Morris's version (which is rarely published now) may be due to Hunt's appropriation and alteration of the stanza.

Spring.
Spring am I, too soft of heart
Much to speak ere I depart:
Ask the Summer-tide to prove
The abundance of my love.

---

1 Lasner, p. 22.
2 Stanley Weintraub, *Four Rossettis* (London: W H Lane, 1978), p. 122.
3 William Morris, *Poems by the Way* (Kelmscott Press, 1891), p. 123.

Summer.
Summer looked for long am I;
Much shall change or e'er I die.
Prithee take it not amiss
Though I weary thee with bliss.

Autumn.
Laden Autumn here I stand
Worn of heart, and weak of hand:
Naught but rest seems good to me,
Speak the word that sets me free.

Winter.
I am Winter, that do keep
Longing safe amidst of sleep:
Who shall say if I were dead
What should be remembered?

I care not for my Ladys soul

I care not for my Ladys soul
Though I worship before her smile
I care not wheres my Ladys goal
When her beauty shall [lose its wile]

Low sit I down at my Ladys feet   5
Gazing through her wild eyes,
Smiling to think how my love will fleet
When their starlike beauty dies

I care not if my Lady pray
To our Father which art in Heaven: 10
Though for joy in my heart wild pulses play
For to me her love is given

Then who shall close my Lady's eyes,
And who shall fold her hands?
Will any hearken if she cries   15
Up to the unknown lands?

Notes

Line 1: The formal language of the poem, referring throughout to "my Lady", recalls poems of courtly love.
Line 3: WMR's version has "where be my Lady's goal".
Line 4: This line is incomplete in the MS. The words used by WMR to complete the line are added in square brackets for ease of reading.
Line 6: The Lady's "wild eyes" indicate a form of repressed madness. Edgar

Allan Poe's "Ligeia", with which the Rossettis, at least, were certainly familiar, is described as having "wild eyes", which indicate not only her own personality but the obsessive nature of the lover, and foretell her early death.[1]

Line 10: Phrasing "our Father which art in Heaven" is taken directly from the Lord's Prayer. WMR amends this to "which is in Heaven".

Line 11: WMR's version read: "But for joy my heart's quick pulses play".

Lines 13-14: Closing the eyes and folding the hands indicate traditional post-mortem rituals.

The poem first appeared in *RRP*, p. 155, under the title "The Lust of the Eyes", a phrase taken from 1 John 2:16: "For all that is in the world, the lust of the flesh, and the lust of the eyes, and the pride of life, is not of the Father, but is of the world." The Bryson MSS includes a fair copy by WMR and an incomplete draft by Siddall. The draft contains virtually no punctuation at all, not even possessive apostrophes, and reads as a more naïve and simple work as a result, an effect that is perhaps misleading.

The poem consists of four four-line stanzas in very irregular metre, although the poem's appearance belies this complexity. The rhyme scheme, however, is very regular and rather conventional, apart from in the third stanza. The metre throughout lurches from iambic to trochaic with frequent substitutions, catalexes and enjambments, yet in reading aloud it has a strange rhythmic music which gives the poem its power. The poem's language complements this: "my Lady" is a very courtly, medieval way of referring to a beloved, yet also somewhat formal, which suits the poem which demonstrates that this love is empty and transient. The irony of a man who loves only for "starlike beauty", and sits at her feet and gazes on her whilst knowing he will move on, has not been lost on biographers who see this poem as a direct representation of the relationship between Siddall and DGR. Hawkesley's biography sees the poem as proof that Rossetti and Siddall consummated their relationship before their marriage, reading it as purely personal.[2] Since we have no date for its composition this is only speculative, and the poem's historical

---

1 Edgar Allan Poe, "Ligeia", pp. 62-78, in *The Fall of the House of Usher and Other Writings* (London: Penguin, 2003), ed. David Galloway, p. 67.

2 Lucinda Hawksley, *Lizzie Siddal: the Tragedy of a Pre-Raphaelite Supermodel* (London: André Deutsch, 2004), pp. 61-2.

element of courtly love seems more stylized than personal, though as
Arcara points out, the poem is able to

> deconstruct with amazing lucidity and bitter irony the relationship
> between model and painter, to the extent of denouncing the objectifying
> gaze of the male artist: from these verses it is clear that Siddal was very
> aware that, as a woman in an artistic environment, she had to confront
> the centrality of an idealized or eroticized femininity, the eternal object
> of enjoyment in androcentric aesthetics.[3]

The first two stanzas construct the Lady as passive, a woman who sits
being admired, with her "wild eyes" alone giving a clue to the personality
that hides beneath her beauty. The third stanza comments on the man's
disregard for her soul, and the last two lines appear to refer to the death
of the Lady in phrases which are very reminiscent of CGR's "When I am
Dead my Dearest". The final stanza, the most regular in metre and the
most peaceful, begins by referring to the Lady's death, asking who will care
for her when she dies, while the last two lines seem to jump backwards to
her life, asking "Will any hearken if she cries/ Up to the unknown lands?"
It is only in these two lines that the Lady with the wild eyes becomes
active: the aestheticised woman has a voice, the poem finally implies, and
one which may even receive an answer. The structure of the poem means
that it is even possible that the cry for help comes after death, permitting
the Lady, like several of CGR's narrators, to speak and act after death
though silenced by convention in life. It is significant, though, that
Siddall's narrator does speak; like CGR's "Monna Innominata", she is
no passive doll. Siddall's is a poem which resists easy consumption of the
female form, suggesting a firm resistance to romantic advances. Hassett
points out that the Lady is not passive or sexually innocent,[4] however; she
is no Lady of Shalott, Mariana or the waiting girl in CGR's "The Prince's
Progress". This Lady is mute but not necessarily a victim.

The poem is often read alongside CGR's "In an Artist's Studio",
which is read as a description of DGR painting Siddall as "One face
looks out from all his canvases"; the poem constructs an almost vampiric
relationship between artist and sitter:

---

3 Stefania Arcara, "Sleep and Liberation: the Opiate World of Elizabeth Siddal",
in Béatrice Laurent (ed.), *Sleeping Beauties in Victorian Britain: Cultural, Literary
and Artistic Explorations of a Myth* (Bern: Peter Lang, 2014), pp. 95-120 (p. 110)
4 Hassett, p. 462.

He feeds upon her face by day and night,
And she with true kind eyes looks back on him,
Fair as the moon and joyful as the light:
Not wan with waiting, not with sorrow dim;
Not as she is, but was when hope shone bright;
Not as she is, but as she fills his dream. (ll. 1-6)

Siddall's poem can therefore be read as an alternative approach to this relationship between artist and muse: the speaker knows the unkindness of his behaviour. The poem is set up to mock the tradition of courtly love, exposing the emptiness of love which relies upon youth and beauty. It is a common enough theme, that love may not last when beauty is gone, and one which "Monna Innominata" also addresses, replacing love with silence:

Youth gone and beauty gone, what doth remain?
The longing of a heart pent up forlorn,
A silent heart whose silence loves and longs;
The silence of a heart which sang its songs
While youth and beauty made a summer morn,
Silence of love that cannot sing again. (14 ll. 9-14)

"Monna Innominata" indicates a weary resignation to the fallibility of male love, but it also consciously permits the woman on a pedestal, the woman-as-muse, to speak, as CGR's introductory words make clear. The distant and fragile relationship again echoes Dante and Beatrice: "Monna Innominata" is a female response to this relationship which permits the silenced woman a voice; Siddall maintains the woman's silence to the end of the poem, but undercuts this silence with irony.

It is not now a longing year

It is not now a longing year
That parts us, not a day,
Yet the green leaves touch me on the cheek
Dear Christ this month of May,
Yet who can take their first dear love   5
and kiss him the old way?

A shadow falls along the grass
and lingers at my feet,
a new face lies between my hands
Dear Christ if I could weep   10
Tears to blot out the summer leaves
when this new face I greet

Still it is but the memory
of something I have seen
In the clammy summer weather   15
When the green leaves came between
The shadow of my dear loves face
So far and strange it seems.

The river ever running down
between its grassy bed   20
The voices of a thousand birds
That clang above my head
Shall bring to me another dream
When this sad dream is dead

Notes

The poem above is taken from the most complete MS of this poem in Siddall's handwriting. However, it differs considerably from the version published by WMR, and there are a number of alternative stanzas on separate pieces of paper in the Bryson and Getty MSS. The Getty MS has an alternative (possibly earlier) draft of the first stanza:[1]

> How days have grown into a year
> Sad hours that bring the day.
> Since I could take my first dear Love
> And kiss him the old way
> Still the green leaves touch me on the cheek
> Dear Christ this month of May

One of the fragments of the Bryson MS contains another version:

> It is not now a longing year,
> That parts us, nor a day
> Yet the green leaves touch me on the cheek,
> Dear Christ this month of May
> and I cannot take my first dear love
> and kiss him the old way.

Line 3: "green leaves" is a phrase repeated several times in this poem. It recalls the words of ballads such as "Barbara Allen", which has a refrain of "when the green leaves were a-falling".
Line 7: A slightly different version of this appears in the Bryson MS:

> A shadow falls along my arms
> And lingers at my feet
> a new face lies between my hands,
> and yet I cannot weep,

---

1 "Rossetti Album (miscellaneous collection, Getty/Wormsley Library)", *The Complete Writings and Pictures of Dante Gabriel Rossetti*, edited by Jerome J. McGann, http://www.rossettiarchive.org/docs/gettymsbook.rad.html, pp. 39-40 [accessed 31.07.17].

So our ~~God~~ Christ has not forgotten me
Since this new face I greet

Line 15: "summer weather" is significant in CGR's "Goblin Market",
where it is repeated several times.
Line 18: "so long" excised and replaced with "so far".
Following this are two excised lines: "Time that shall wither the green
leaves/Shall dull this heart of mine."
Line 22: The version which appears in the Getty MS has "sing" instead
of "clang", while line 23 has "sudden" instead of "another", though
elsewhere in the Bryson MS this appears as "sadder", so this may be a
transcription error.

A further, substantial draft exists in the Bryson collection, which
formed the basis of the DGR fair copy:

Slow days have passed that make a year
Slow hours that make a day,
Since I could take my first dear love
And kiss him the old way,
Yet the green leaves touch me on the cheek   5
Dear Christ this month of May.

A shadow falls along the grass
And [illegible] it at my feet
A new face lies between my hands
Dear Christ if I weep   10
Tears to shut out the summer leaves
When this new face I greet

Dim phantoms of an unknown ill
Float through my tired brain
The unformed visions of my life   15
Pass by in ghostly train
Some pause to touch me on the cheek

Some scatter tears like rain

A silence falls upon my heart
And hushes all its pain,   20
I stretch my hands in the long grass
And fall to sleep again,
There to lie empty of all love
Like beaten corn of grain

The indication in the last line is that the nourishing kernel of the grain has been removed; corn stalks were traditionally beaten to remove the corn for use.

Further stanzas appear in fragmented form in the Bryson collection:

Dim phamptoms [sic] of an unknown ill
Float through my tired brain
The unformed visions of my life
of my life
Pass by in ghastly train
Some linger with a loving look
some scatter tears like rain

A further alternative version:

Dim phantoms of
some unknown ill
Float through my tired brain
The unfounded visions
of my life pass by in ghastly train
some pause to touch me on the cheek
some scatter tears like rain

WMR's version has "tiring brain". The line "Dim phantoms of an unknown ill" is one of the most-quoted lines of Siddall's poetry, frequently used to indicate her precarious mental state. "Dim phantoms" is a term that appears occasionally in nineteenth-century writing, particularly writing about psychological states, however. For example, it appears in *The Dublin University Magazine* in 1835: "The hallucinations of delirium and the dim phantoms of dreaming have been traced into an affinity with the phenomena of mental aberration by many writers upon this latter subject."[2] Coleridge writes in "Self-Knowledge" of "A phantom dim of past and future wrought". It is a phrase which writers as diverse as Felicia Hemans and Elizabeth Gaskell use, suggesting it had some currency in the period in which Siddall was writing.

A further stanza also appears among the Bryson fragments:

I lie among the tall green grass
That bends above my head

And covers up my wasted face,
And folds me in its bed
Tenderly and lovingly
Like grass above the dead.

Like CGR's "When I am Dead, my Dearest", the speaker is simulating death: "Be the green grass above me/With showers and dewdrops wet" (ll. 5-6). The Getty MS has "spreads above my head"; a separate Bryson MS has "cheeks" instead of "face".

A further fragment appears in the Bryson MSS which is almost certainly a part of this poem:

Time that shall dry
The river bed
and hush the song of birds
Shall stop the pulses of the heart
where sorry has no words

The subject, language and rhythm of these lines indicate the probability of it being a part of this poem, especially since it appears on a sheet with

---

2 *Dublin University Magazine: A Literary and Political Journal*, vol. 6, December 1835, "Some Effects of Unnoticed Insanity", (p. 666-675), p. 666, anonymous

the lines "The river ever running down/between its grassy bed/That clang above my head/shall bring to me a sadder [paper torn]/When this sad dream is dead".

Yet another scrap reads:

The Wind is heavy[?] with
the sound of song Birds
and hush
The river running ever down
between its grassy bed
Now you come
Love poured into the heavy
heart is dull and dead.

For comparison, the version published by WMR is given below:

A Year and a Day

Slow days have passed that make a year,
Slow hours that make a day,
Since I could take my first dear love,
And kiss him the old way:
Yet the green leaves touch me on the cheek,
Dear Christ, this month of May.

I lie among the tall green grass
That bends above my head,
And covers up my wasted face,
And folds me in its bed
Tenderly and lovingly
Like grass above the dead.

Dim phantoms of an unknown ill
Float through my tiring brain;
The unformed visions of my life
Pass by in ghostly train:

Some pause to touch me on the cheek,
Some scatter tears like rain.

The river ever running down
Between its grassy bed,
The voices of a thousand birds
That clang above my head,
Shall bring to me a sadder dream
When this sad dream is dead.

A silence falls upon my heart,
And hushes all its pain.
I stretch my hands in the long grass,
And fall to sleep again,
There to lie empty of all love,
Like beaten corn of grain.

This poem, perhaps Siddall's most famous, which often appears in anthologies, was first published in *FLM* by WMR (pp. 176-7). It was the first poem to be published, with several stanzas omitted from WMR's version. "A year and a day", the title he gives it, has connotations of a mythical or symbolic period of time, such as might be found in a fairy-tale or ballad. In *The Wife of Bath*, the Knight is given a year and a day to discover what women most desire, for example. The ballad "The Unquiet Grave" contains the lines "I'll sit and mourn all at her grave/For a twelvemonth and a day." "A year and a day" also has legal significance; the "year and a day rule" required that a victim die within 366 days of an attack for the accused to be considered guilty of murder.

This is Siddall's longest poem, and the extent to which she worked on it and developed it is apparent from the number of drafts extant. The Ashmolean fair copy by DGR, with a note saying "Omit this poem" (Bryson 2599d) forms the basis of the WMR version; there are also a number of drafts in Siddall's handwriting. Two slightly different stanzas appear on the back of a letter to Emma Madox Brown (reproduced in Appendix 1). Different versions of some stanzas are also in holograph form in the Getty collection (see notes on poem); these are monographed EES. The problems of arriving at a final form of this poem are many:

the fragments give no indication of authorial intention, since they are undated, which is why the DGR fair copy has taken precedence, and punctuation and spelling, as well as word choice, vary from fragment to fragment. However, it is fascinating to trace the development of the poem, if not chronologically, by considering the drafts, as this indicates how seriously Siddall took her writing. This poem is very significant, therefore, for demonstrating the complexities of a poet's working practice: the development of phrases and stanzas is apparent, and tracing through the fragments it is possible to see the ways in which she has come up with a better way of expressing a thought, or a more appropriate scansion for a line. It is also clear that she worked in a haphazard way, though, from the verses written on the back of the letter to Emma Madox Brown.

The poem indicates a mourning of the dead (or lost), as well as implying a longing for death, as Angeli suggests so many of Siddall's poems do. The phrasing is reminiscent of traditional ballads, and without using archaic language, the poem is constructed in an apparently simple, faux-medieval style. Yet the speaker takes up a complex position: as Arcara writes:

> In a very similar manner to Christina Rossetti, Siddal creates a poetic mood of forgetting and disenchantment. She refuses the conventional role of woman as love-victim by strategically taking refuge in a remote space of resistance and isolation, that of sleep, in the liminality between life and death.[3]

The surface simplicity is consequently deceptive; this is a well-crafted poem which demonstrates Siddall's commitment to and understanding of poetic form. She writes in alternating tetrameter and trimeter lines, commonly known as hymn metre, in six-line stanzas, with substitutions which play to the content of the poem. For example, the opening line "Slow days have passed that make a year" begins with a spondaic substitution, slowing the reader down and using the metre to play with time just as the poem itself does.

The speaker of the poem allies herself with the natural world in order to protect herself from misery, a common trope of Siddall's poetry: the "tall green grass" is conjured as if for its restorative effects. Another effect which appears frequently in her work is the "summer leaves", which seem to heighten the speaker's anguish. Violet Hunt, however, allies the poem

---

3 Arcara, p. 117.

entirely with Siddall's mental state:

> the verses which she posted to him began to show a less terrible mental oscillation than they had done. They suggested more the sobbing sleep of a child that has been affronted by its elders, half-pacified, half-angry still.[4]

Arcara, by contrast, suggests there is something more rebellious and less sentimental at work in this poem:

> The dreaming woman in "A Year and a Day" is a disobedient Sleeping Beauty, not the damsel waiting for romantic salvation, but a self-contained creature practising indifference.[5]

The alternative versions and stanzas included above bear this out, offering less resignation than WMR's final compilation of texts suggests.

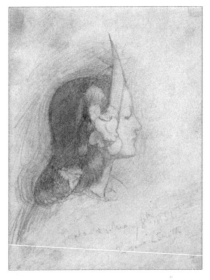

Image 3: Barbara Leigh Smith Bodichon, Elizabeth Siddall, pencil on paper, 1854 (Mark Samuels Lasner Collection, on loan to the University of Delaware Library)

---

4 Violet Hunt, *The Wife of Rossetti; Her Life and Death, etc* (London: John Lane, 1932), p. 193
5 Arcara, p. 118

Life and night are falling from me

Life and night are falling
from me, Death are
opening on me
Where ever my footsteps
come and go life is a   5
stony way of woe
Lord have I long to go

Hollow hearts are ever
near me soulless eyes have
ceased to cheer me   10
Lord may I come to Thee

Life and youth and summer
weather to my heart no joy
can gather
Lord lift me from life's stony way   15

Loved eyes long closed in death
wach for me holy death is
waiting for me
Lord may I come today

My outward life feels sad   20
and still like lilies in
a frozen rill

I am gazing upwards to the
sun Lord Lord remembering
my lost one   25
Oh Lord remember me

How is it in the unknown
land do the dead wander
hand in hand
give me trust in thee   30

Do we clasp dead hands
and quiver with an endless
joy for ever
good be unto thee

Is the air filled with   35
wail [illegible] of spirits circling
round and round

Is the air filled with harp
[illegible] to fasten our angels wings
upon   40

are there lakes of endless
song to rest our tired eyes
upon

Do tall white angels
gaze and wend along   45
the banks where lilies
bend

Lord we know not how
this may be good Lord
we put our faith in thee   50
Oh God remember me

Notes

This incomplete text is taken from the Ashmolean draft.

Line 2: sic. Siddall's grammar is often idiosyncratic.

Line 6: The concept of life as a stony path is a common one: in David Copperfield (1849-50), for example, Dickens writes that his path in life "is stony and rugged now". The concept of a stony place or path being unfruitful and difficult to cross recurs in the Bible, and forms the central trope of Bunyan's *The Pilgrim's Progress* (1678).

Lines 12-13: "summer weather" offers no comfort in several of Siddall's poems. As with CGR's work, nature's ability to comfort is limited in the face of life's trials, and spiritual love is the only true consolation.

Line 17: sic

Line 21: Lilies have significance in Christian belief as a symbol of chastity and innocence, and were used in early Christian art to depict the Virgin Mary. Their beauty is referred to in the Bible (see Luke 12:27, for example). They are also traditionally associated with death. These lilies are frozen, preserving their beauty forever.

Line 26: Siddall's prayerful invocations echo Biblical words. Here, her plea seems to summon the words of Luke 23:42-43: "And he said unto Jesus, Lord, remember me when thou comest into thy kingdom. And Jesus said unto him, Verily I say unto thee, To day shalt thou be with me in paradise." "Dear" is excised and replaced with "Oh".

Lines 28-33: Revelation 21.4 imagines a similar vision of perfect happiness: "And God shall wipe away all tears from their eyes; and there shall be no more death, neither sorrow, nor crying, neither shall there be any more pain: for the former things are passed away."

Line 40: Two excised stanzas here read:

Do tall white angels [illegible]
along the lily [illegible] banks

of song

Do tall white angels come
and go along the banks
were [sic] lilies grow

Line 45: "wend" is an unusually archaic word for this poem, probably
chosen for its rhyme, though, in conjunction with the lilies mentioned, it
presents a medievalized Pre-Raphaelite image.
Below, for comparison, is WMR's version, from *SR* 1. Other
subsequently published versions contain slightly different spacing and
punctuation.

Life and night are falling from me,
Death and day are opening on me.
Wherever my footsteps come and go
Life is a stony way of woe.
Lord, have I long to go?   5
Hollow hearts are ever near me,
Soulless eyes have ceased to cheer me:
Lord, may I come to thee?
Life and youth and summer weather
To my heart no joy can gather: 10
Lord, lift me from life's stony way.
Loved eyes, long closed in death, watch o'er me –
Holy Death is waiting for me –
Lord, may I come to-day?
My outward life feels sad and still,   15
Like lilies in a frozen rill.
I am gazing upwards to the sun,
Lord, Lord, remembering my lost one.
O Lord, remember me!
How is it in the unknown land?

Do the dead wander hand in hand?
Do we clasp dead hands, and quiver
With an endless joy for ever?
Is the air filled with the sound
Of spirits circling round and round?   25
Are there lakes, of endless song,
To rest our tirèd eyes upon?
Do tall white angels gaze and wend
Along the banks where lilies bend?
Lord, we know not how this may be;   30
Good Lord we put our faith in thee –
O God, remember me.

This poem was first published in *SR* (pp. 199-200); the Ashmolean draft is monogrammed EER. Both versions of the poem are provided here, since the textual variants are considerable: Siddall's is clearly incomplete and irregular, and drafts of other poems indicate that given time she may well have worked further on this. However, her draft is worth printing, since it indicates a very different rhythm and approach from WMR's tidied-up text.

Lasner comments:

Early 1862. WMR is quite definite about this MS., "written in a very shaky and straggling way; I surmise that it must have been done under the influence of laudanum … and probably not long before her death." Tradition has it that DGR found these verses near his dying wife. Possibly "my lost one" (stanza 4) refers to her daughter. WMR thinks that the "loved eyes" of the previous stanza are those of a brother who had died before she met DGR.[1]

Titled "Lord May I Come?" by WMR, this is in some ways a more complex poem than many of Siddall's other poems. Opening with the line "Life and night are falling from me", it takes the unusual approach of coupling life with darkness. The internal rhymes of "life" and "night" help to integrate contrasting ideas so that they might almost pass without comment. The words "falling" and "opening" suggests that the transition

---

1 Lasner, p. 22.

between life and death will be an easy one, and the stanza suggests that life will be happily left behind. The first two lines are strong, regularly phrased and using a double-rhyme of "me". The next three lines are uneven, the word "wherever" causing the reading to stumble as though themselves on a "stony way of woe". The remaining stanzas seem to follow a similar pattern, with some repeated rhymes, and the constant questioning, and occasionally a substitution which makes the reader pay attention, for example the repeated "Lord, Lord, remembering my lost one", where the double emphasis adds to the pathos of the poem. WMR, in *SR*, reads the poem biographically as one of personal melancholy:

> There is a wail of pang and pathos in it not readily forgettable. Indeed, one of the most noticeable points in her verses generally (I will not say uniformly) is their excessive and seldom-relieved melancholy - a "darkness that can be felt." It is however a melancholy which to some extent merges into a future hope the sense of settled desolation in this world. The verses give more evidence of a certain spiritual faith, pervasive though undefined, than I ever heard in the writer's conversation.[2]

The repeated questions form a pleasing pattern with which to frame the poem. Though it is a poem of sadness, in many ways, referring to a bereavement and the melancholy of life, it is not a poem without hope. The speaker is "gazing upwards to the sun" like a lily in frozen water; she has hope, though not exactly optimism. The speaker is asking for reassurance, and the questions she asks are characteristic of her contemporaries: "How long?", "How is it in the unknown land?" In the penultimate stanza, the speaker prays for trust in God; and the final stanza suggests her prayers have been answered. In this respect in particular, the poem could be mistaken for one of CGR's; it is structurally simple but effective, and it is possible that Siddall was inspired by Rossetti's poetics and even faith, though Siddall does have her own unique touches, such as the medievalism of her aesthetics and directness of language, which Rossetti does not manifest to any great extent. Like Rossetti, though, the poem uses the personal pronoun to permit the words to be associated with the reader, turning it into a kind of prayer with an appealing universality. This use of "I" in a poem is common in nineteenth-century

2 William Michael Rossetti (ed.), *Some Reminiscences*, 2 vols (New York: Scribner, 1906), p.196.

poetry, particularly devotional poems, and consequently cannot be read as personal to the poet.

The speaker also asks, "Do the dead wander hand in hand?" A desire for reunion with loved ones in heaven is a notable preoccupation not only of CGR's work but also of many other writers, and the memory of the dead was a powerful force for the Victorians, formalised in elaborate mourning rituals and taken to extremes with spiritualism and séances, with which Siddall was familiar. There is something almost other-worldly about the images of this poem, too: the final stanza offers a Pre-Raphaelite image of conventional Christianity superimposed on nature. Marsh suggests that this poem contain echoes of "The Blessed Damozel", though she comments that these lines contain "an original and vivid image of ghostly lovers".[3] The "tall white angels" are distinctly reminiscent of a Pre-Raphaelite aesthetic with its stylised medievalism, and despite the slightly strained archaism of "wend" the lines have an unusual beauty which seems to be purely decorative.

---

3 Marsh, *The Legend of Elizabeth Siddal*, p. 203.

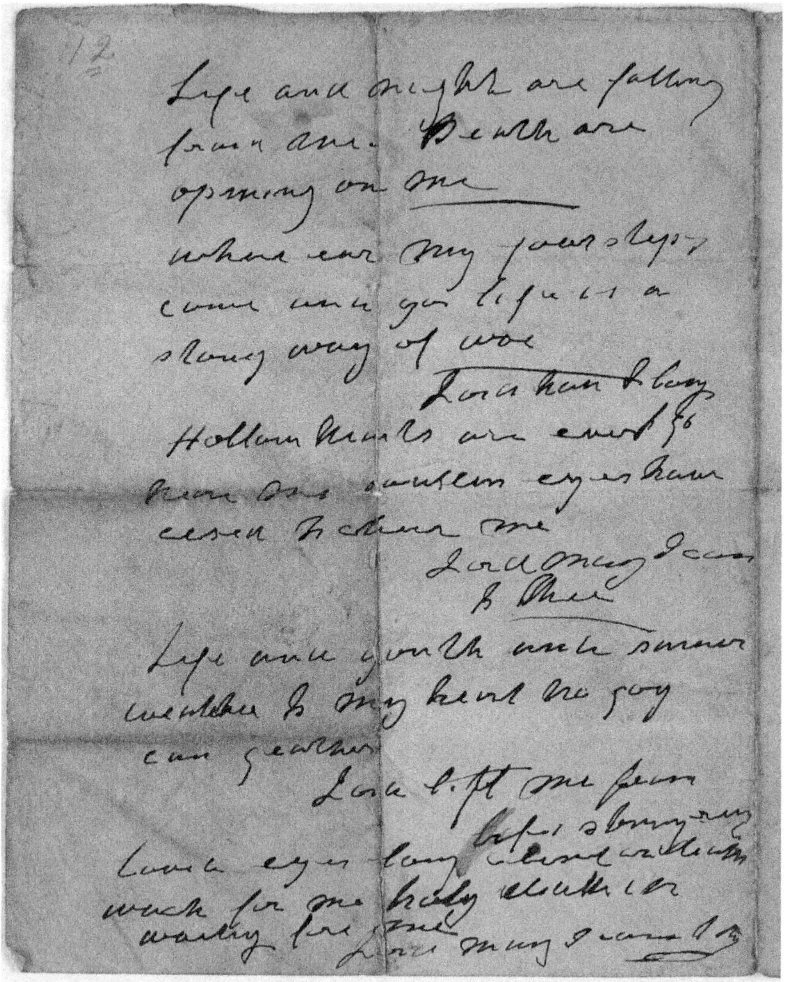

Image 4: MS "Life and night are falling from me", Ashmolean Museum, WA1977.182, Image © Ashmolean Museum, University of Oxford

Many a mile over land and sea

1
Many a mile over land and sea
Unsummoned my love returned to me
I remember not the words he said
But only the trees moaning over head

2
And he came ready to take and bear   5
The cross I had carried for many a year
But words came slowly one by one
from frozen lips shut still and dumb

3
How sounded my words so still and slow
To the great strong heart that loved me so   10
Who came to save from pain and wrong
and comfort me with a love so strong

4
Ah I remember my God so well
My brain lie dumb in a frozen spell
and I looked away from my lovers face   15
to watch the dead leaves that were running apace

5
I felt the wind strike chill and cold
and vapours rise from the red brown mould

I felt the spell that held my breath
Bending me down to a living death   20

6
As if hope lie bruised when he had come
who knew my sorrows one by one
and until comfort and pity [two illegible words]
and give me the help of his own right hand

Notes

Line 2: The unsummoned lover returning from beyond the grave is a common trope in Romantic poetry, and one which DGR and CGR also explore (for example, in CGR's "The Hour and the Ghost". The inspiration for this and other poems may have been Gottfried Bürger's poem "Lenore", which the Rossettis read as children.)

Lines 5-6: This has connotations of the Christian notion of disciples of Christ metaphorically "bearing the cross" (Matthew 10: 38-39). In what way the "unsummoned" lover might lift the speaker's burden is unclear, but with his "great strong heart" and ability to save in the subsequent stanza, the implication is that this spectral visitor may even represent Christ.

Line 8: The concept of being frozen and unable to move or speak is common in Siddall's poems; see, for example, "O silent wood I enter thee".

Line 13: An excised line in the MS reads "Ah I remember so well". In the rewritten line, "how" is excised and replaced with "so".

Line 14: sic. As with line 21, this is Siddall's word choice.

Line 16: WMR's fair copy replaces "running apace" with "running a race".

Line 18: "And" replaces the excised words "I still".

Line 20: The "living death" is represented by the frozen inability to speak, a similar trope as is used in "O silent wood I enter thee".

WMR fair copy:

Speechless

Many a mile o'er land and sea
Unsummoned my love returned to me;
I remember not the words he said,
But only the trees mourning overhead.
And he came ready to take and bear   5
The cross I had carried for many a year:
But my words came slowly one by one
From frozen lips that were still and dumb.
How sounded my words so still and slow
To the great strong heart that loved me so?   10
Ah I remember, my God, so well,
How my brain lay dumb in a frozen spell;
And I leaned away from my lover's face
To watch the dead leaves that were running a race.
I felt the spell that held my breath,   15
Bending me down to a living death –
As if hope lay buried when he had come
Who knew my sorrows all and some.

The Bryson bequest contains both a fair copy by WMR and an incomplete draft by Siddall.[1] This version of the poem is taken from Siddall's unfinished MS. A number 7 follows the poem, indicating her intention to write another stanza, and a note in her handwriting on the page reads "see to this". Siddall's poem is in her usual 4-line stanzaic form, in rhyming couplets. Her layout makes this much clearer than in WMR's version, which eliminates the stanzaic form.

The poem was first printed in *RRP* (p. 154) under the title "Speechless". Hawksley suggests that an alternative title is "Sleepless", however, and believes that it may be one of her earliest poems, possibly written around 1854, though no source is given for this.[2] It is most frequently referred

1 WMR fair copy 2599h; Siddall draft WA1977.182.6.
2 Hawksley, p. 55.

to as "Fragment of a Ballad". It is one of Siddall's most dramatic and
haunting poems, and her draft offers a naïve source of power which is
toned down in WMR's version (as was possibly his intention).

The poem's atmosphere of menace and haunting is reminiscent of
some of CGR's ghost poems, and evokes an atmosphere redolent of "A
Coast-Nightmare", in which "a friend" returns to tell the narrator of his
experience of death. Marsh reads the poem as a narrative of a failed rescue:
"this prince has come too late: he cannot revive his princess" – recalling
CGR's "The Prince's Progress", in which the laggardly prince arrives,
dawdling, after the death of the princess.[3] Yet the figure of the "lover"
is hardly a fairy-tale prince, as Marsh is aware: "Is the rescuer 'with his
love so strong' a human figure, or perhaps Christ the Saviour, 'ready to
take and bear / The cross I had carried', or rather Death itself, with his
fatal yet welcome embrace?"[4] Hawksley is sure that this vampiric lover is
DGR himself, but we can only speculate.[5] The language used does seem
to point to a dark, Christ-like figure, however, especially concluding with
the previously unpublished stanza with its line "and give me the help of
his own right hand".

3 Marsh, *The Legend of Elizabeth Siddal*, p. 211.
4 Marsh, *The Legend of Elizabeth Siddal*, p. 211.
5 Hawksley, p. 56, p. 60.

Now Christ ye save yon bonny shepherd

Now Christ ye save yon bonny shepherd
Sailing on the sea,
Ten thousand souls are sailing there
But they belong to Thee.
If he is lost then all is lost   5
and all is dead to me.

My love should have a grey head stone
And green grass at his feet
And clinging grass above his breast
Whereon his lambs could bleat,   10
And I should know the span of earth
Where some day I might sleep.

Notes

Line 1: WMR's version opens: "Now Christ thee save, thou bonny Shepherd". Folksongs contain many "bonny shepherds", such as the Scottish ballad "Young Beichan and Susie Pye"[1]
Line 3: The phrase "ten thousand souls" is also a familiar one, with implications of biblical or folkloric history. Daniel Herbert's hymn "Ten Thousand Souls" (published 1815) is one example; it also features in theological writing of the period, and appears in countless prayers and Christian rhetoric. Deuteronomy 33.2 refers to "ten thousand saints".
Line 4: WMR's version: "But I belong to thee."
Line 5: WMR's version: "If thou art lost"
Line 8: WMR's version: "green moss".

---

1   Jamieson, Robert, ed., *Popular Ballads and Songs, from Tradition, Manuscripts, and Scarce Editions* (Edinburgh: John Murray, 1806), pp. 117-126.

Line 12: WMR's version omits "Where".

This poem, given the title "Shepherd Turned Sailor" by WMR, was first published in *RRP*, pp. 152-3. The Ashmolean fair copy is in DGR's hand, along with a draft by Siddall, which is replicated here. Marsh (1991) also uses the version above, while other published versions, in print and online, frequently use variants of both texts.

The scansion and phrasing of the poem gives it a traditional, balladic tone. The repeated words (lost ... lost and all ... all in lines 5-6, for example) provide emphasis and an internal structure. The poem reads as a prayer for sailors, but for one in particular, the "bonny shepherd", who is perhaps a lover or son.

Siddall's fascination with the sea, which she had never seen before her first trip to Hastings with DGR in 1852, is documented by biographers. Victorian poetry is saturated with images of the sea, its power and ability to take lives; it appears as a metaphor for the act of death (such as in Tennyson's "Crossing the Bar") and for the besetting anxieties of the period (in Matthew Arnold's "Dover Beach"). It appears in many contemporary works of literature and art as a source of sadness; the Newlyn painter Walter Langley (1852-1922), for example, painted many pictures of women grieving for dead sailors, and it is this tradition that this short ballad seems to echo. The poem is also thematically linked to her other poems, of course, in its mourning for a lost lover and its acknowledgement of coming death. It is striking that the poem describes the sailor's ultimate place of rest; like CGR, Siddall is interested in burial, aligning the returning of the body to the earth with natural imagery ("green grass", "lambs", in this poem), permitting the speaker a calm resignation to death as life, in the form of nature, will go on regardless.

O god forgive me that I ranged

O god forgive me that I ranged
My life into a dream of love
Will tears of anguish never wash
the passion from my blood.

Love kept my heart in a song of joy   5
My pulses quivered to the tune
The coldest blasts of winter blew
upon me like sweet airs in June

Love floated on the mists of morn
and rested on the sunsets rays   10
He calmed the thunder of the storm
and lighted all my ways

O Heaven help my foolish heart
which heeded not the passing time
that dragged my idol from its place   15
and shattered all its shrine

Love held me joyful through the day
and dreaming all through the night
No evil thing could come to me
my spirit was so light   20

Notes

A note on the back of the MS reads: "Oh God I ranged my life into a dream of love".

Line 1: WMR's version replaces "ranged" with "merged". The writing is scrawled, and either reading is possible.

Line 3: Bryson MS contains the crossed-out word "away" at the end of this line, with "never" inserted above it. The concept of washing away past pain with tears is a familiar trope, and appears in the Bible in Luke 7:38, in which a Pharisee woman washes Jesus's feet with her tears in a reflection of the spiritual cleansing of baptism.

Line 7: "coldest blasts of winter" recalls CGR's "Winter: My Secret", in which she teases the reader with her layers and will not explain her meaning. Such a reading is perhaps appropriate here, too, since the poem is so often presumed to be biographical.

Line 13: The last two verses appear the other way around in WMR's published version. This is presumably because he felt that some sense of closure might be reached by the penultimate stanza, asking for help from Heaven. However, the uncertainty and return to reflection on the joys of love by Siddall's final stanza is worth noting.

Line 14: "That" is crossed out and replaced with "which".

Line 15: The concept of a fallen idol is a familiar one, originating in the Bible, particularly 1 Samuel 5. The concept appears in several poems: CGR writes in "Memory" that a choice she made was "Breaking mine idol" (l. 15), while more obscurely, the poet Amanda Corey Edmond, a friend of Longfellow's, wrote in 1845 in her poem "Christ is Left": "Clinging to each shattered shrine,/Of its idol sweet bereft,/Never can my soul repine,/While it grieves – if Christ is left."

Line 18: WMR's version reads "dreaming ever through the night".

This poem was first published by WMR in *SR*. The Ashmolean draft is slightly different, and it is this monogrammed draft which is printed here. The poem consists of five four-line stanzas; in *SR* the last two are transposed, which perhaps concludes the poem in a more final way, but the draft, with a more positive conclusion, ends with a reflection on the joys of love and its ability to protect the lover from evil. As Hassett points out,

On occasion, Siddal creates a lover who is less diffident, one who celebrates before she mourns in "The Passing of Love." As she tells of how "Love" light-heartedly "floated on the mists of morn, / And rested on the sunset's rays," Siddal subdues the middle stresses to lighten the rhythm as well. Against this delicate buoyancy, time and tempo work their dire effects and disillusionment sets in with emphatic lines that alliterate their transitive verbs.[1]

The poem has a striking regularity, in rhythm and rhyme as well as in its alliteration and the words which start each stanza (3 begin with "Love", the other two "O God" and "O Heaven"). The emphasis shifts between despair at the ending of love, and remembered joy at the happiness it brought. Like her other poems, this is often related to Siddall's relationship with Rossetti, but regardless of the origin of the concept it is a poem which is carefully crafted and provides a demonstration of her poetic skill.

Each verse provides its own discrete argument which forms one whole; the language of each stanza is subtly varied: stanzas 1 and 4 use biblical language, of "passion" and "blood", "idol" and "shrine", while those which refer to earthly love use the natural world to reflect the joy the speaker feels: the "sweet airs in June" and the "mists of morn". The final stanza uses a different register, that of time, to indicate the timelessness but also the transience of human love.

The poem echoes CGR's work in several ways, but particularly in the demonstration of the failure of earthly love, compared with the everlasting security of divine love, which is a central argument here, and one which CGR manifests throughout her oeuvre. If God provides not exactly solace but a possibility of healing from past psychic wounds, humanity provides earthly joy, though it is finite.

---

1 Hassett, pp. 457-8.

O grieve not with thy bitter tears

1
O grieve not with thy bitter tears
My life that passes so fast
the gates of heaven will open wide
and take me in at last

2
Then sit down meekly at my side   5
and watch my young life flee
Then solemn peace of holy death
Come quickly unto thee

3
But true love seek me in the throng
of spirits floating past   10
and I will take thee by the hands
and know thee mine at last

Notes

Line 1: Some published versions have "Oh".
Line 2: WMR's version reads "The life that passes fast".
Line 10: The "throng/Of spirits" recalls Dante's experiences in Inferno at the beginning of Canto V, where in the Circle of Incontinence those who have committed sins such as adultery are tossed around by violent winds, a metaphor for their storms of passion in life. This was depicted by DGR in "Paolo and Francesca" (1855).
Line 11: This is the reverse of CGR's comment in "Remember", in which "you can no more hold me by the hand" (l.3).

The poem, titled "Early Death" by WMR, first appeared in *SR* vol. I (pp. 196-7).

This restrained, brief poem is one of those which have led critics to conclude that Siddall was obsessed with death, almost willing herself to an early grave. It bears the hallmarks of many of her other poems, however: a strong visual perspective combines with a ballad-like form of rhyming four-line stanzas. The simple, modern language of the poem, eschewing archaisms excepting "thee" and "thy", lends a gentle appeal to the words of the young speaker. While it is easy for modern readers to see this poem as maudlin and melodramatic, the likelihood of early death was much greater in the nineteenth century, of course, and deathbed scenes such as this appear frequently throughout the literature of the period, from Dickens to Charlotte Yonge. Also, of course, as Marsh points out, "Poems which to modern ears seem morbidly to welcome youthful death were popular in the Victorian era".[1]

The speaker exhorts the lover not to grieve, anticipating a happy future in heaven when the lovers will be reunited: the vision of a reunion in heaven is a frequent topic in writings on Victorian mourning, in which whole families might be together again. The biblical precedent for this belies this belief; Luke 20: 34-36 says:

> The children of this world marry, and are given in marriage: But they which shall be accounted worthy to obtain that world, and the resurrection from the dead, neither marry, nor are given in marriage: Neither can they die any more: for they are equal unto the angels; and are the children of God, being the children of the resurrection.

Like "The Blessed Damozel", the temptation artistically to imagine a heavenly reunion is irresistible, constructing death as a temporary separation which is thus more bearable. In fact, Siddall, like CGR, constructs heaven as an improvement upon earth, and consequently spiritual love as superior to earthly love, in its permanency.

---

1   Marsh, *Elizabeth Siddal: Pre-Raphaelite Artist*, p. 31.

O mother open the window wide

O mother open the window wide
and let the daylight in
The Hills grow darker to my sight
and thoughts begin to swim

And mother dear take my young son   5
since I was born of thee
and care for all little ways
and nurse it on your knee

And mother, wash my pale pale hands
and then bind up my feet   10
My body may no longer rest
Out of its winding sheet

And mother dear take a sapling twig
and green grass newly mown,
and lay it on my empty bed   15
that my sorrow be not known

And mother find three berries red
and pluck them from the stalk,
and burn them at the first cockcrow
that my spirit may not walk   20

And mother dear break a willow wand
and if two be even,

Then save it for sweet Roberts sake
and he'll know my souls in heaven

and mother when the big tears fall   25
and fall God knows they may
Tell I died of my great love
and my dying heart was gay

And mother dear when the sun has set
and the pale kirk grass waves   30
Then carry me through the dim twilight
and hide among the graves

Notes

Line 1: An old custom was to open the windows to allow the soul to escape.

Line 7: WMR's version inserts "his" ("and care for all his little ways").

Line 8: WMR's version reads "And nurse him on thy knee".

Line 9: Washing the hands of the dead is symbolic of their sins being washed away, in an echo of baptism.

Line 10: Some folklore suggests that the feet of a corpse be bound to prevent them walking after death. Other superstitions suggest binding them loosely so that they may walk freely into the afterlife.

Line 11: "stay" is excised and replaced with "rest".

Line 14: Hole suggests that "green turf" by the bed of the deceased will prevent evil spirits (similar to the more common dish of salt).

Line 15: WMR's version reads: "lay them"

Line 17: This is likely to refer to rowan berries, which were considered to have protective powers against ghosts and witchcraft, (see Frazer, p. 620) as does holly (Hole, p.88, 91).

Line 21: The mournful "Willow Song" sung by Desdemona in Othello precedes her death (Act IV scene iii); the doomed Ophelia in Hamlet is also associated with willow, whose branch breaks as she enters the water to her death. Some superstitions associate the willow with protection from the devil, which may account for the suggestion here. Alexander suggests that willow "symbolized the pain of lost love" (p319).

Line 22: WMR's version: "if the sap be even"

Line 23: WMR's version reads "my lover's sake". "sweet Robert", who may be the lover or the child, reads like a name from a ballad; Scott's *Minstrelsy* contains many "sweet" or "fair" figures.

Line 27: WMR's version inserts "him" ("tell him I died")

Line 30: WMR's version: "church grass". The "twilight" in the churchyard recalls the "twilight/That doth not rise nor set" in CGR's "song".

Line 32: WMR's version: "hide me among the graves"

This poem first appeared in *RRP* (pp. 240-2). The MS sources are a draft in the Bryson collection, monogrammed EER, with a comment in different handwriting which reads "Not earlier than May 60", and a fair copy by DGR. Published versions of the poem vary in the use of some words but the poem which appears here is taken from the EER draft. WMR states:

> I have separated this poem from others written before Mrs. Dante Rossetti's marriage, because I find her MS. of it (rather roughly done) upon paper bearing the stamped initials E.E.R. It is of course possible that the poem had been written before her marriage, and copied out afterwards; but I have no particular reason for thinking this.[1]

As Lasner points out, this poem may have "an intention at least partly literary, perhaps inspired by old ballads such as 'Lord Randall'".[2] It is frequently linked by biographers to her first pregnancy, relating the topic of the death of a mother (though there is no specific indication that the narrator is dying from childbirth) to Siddall's own fraught pregnancy which ended in miscarriage. Mégroz suggests this poem has connections to Tennyson's "The May Queen" (which he refers to as "May Day").[3] The second part of "The May Queen", "The New Year", relates the wishes of a dying girl related to her mother, including the request to care for her young daughter, opening with the line "If you're waking call me early, call me early, mother dear," and the poems do appear to partake of the same

---

1 William Michael Rossetti (ed.), *Ruskin, Rossetti, Pre-Raphaelitism* (London: Allen, 1899), p. 240.

2 Lasner, p. 24.

3 Mégroz, p. 74.

tradition, although "The May Queen" concludes with the surprising failure of the May Queen to die. The scene depicted by Siddall recalls Frederick Sandys's "The Sailor's Bride" (1860-1), a wood-block engraving to accompany the now-forgotten poem of the same name by Marian E. James, which also has echoes of the ballad tradition in which Siddall is writing:

> Then stole a cloud across her face;
> "All things are growing dim,
> Mother! Can this be death?
> Kiss me, and give my love to him."[4]

Siddall's poem is heavily influenced by traditional ballads, particularly Scott's *Minstrelsy*; Hassett suggests "Clerk Saunders" as a context for the poem, as well as indicating the thematic links to other ballads.[5] The folklore and superstition of the poem is difficult to pin down to specific traditions; Hassett sagely points out that:

> So apparently authentic are these details that the modern reader might readily assume that Siddal borrows "real" Minstrelsy details … But while it is tempting to accept these directives as denotative of the traditional beliefs that are expounded by antiquarians like Walter Scott, they are, in part, Siddal's own invention. Not only do they work brilliantly to create the atmosphere of lykewake superstition and fear, their unfamiliarity is consistent with the lost origin or culturally forgotten "meaning" of many ballad details.[6]

These invented signifiers "display Siddall's artistic confidence and announce her originality".[7] Similarly, the references to the natural world, and the overall theme of preparing for death, suggest the poet's immersion in traditional language and concepts. The poem more or less follows typical ballad form, in 4-line stanzas with four-stress lines followed by 3-stress lines. However, the metre is irregular, and, significantly, the rhyme scheme is looser than in many ballads. This may in part be due to its nature as a draft, but also indicates an ability to play around with the form and experiment in a way which permitted the narrator some immediacy of speech.

---

4 Marion James, "The Sailor's Bride", *Once a Week* (13th April 1861, vol. 4, p. 434)

5 Hassett, p. 452.

6 Hassett, p. 453.

7 Hassett, p. 453.

O silent wood I enter thee

1
O silent wood I enter thee
with a heart so full of misery
For all the voices from the trees
and the ferns that cling about my knees

2
In thy darkest shadow let me sit   5
When the grey owls about me flit
There I will ask of the a boon
That I may not faint or die or swoon

3
Gazing through the gloom like one
Whose life and hopes are also done   10
Frozen like a thing of stone
I sit in thy shadow but not alone

4
Poor spell bound lips that uttered not a word
O frozen heart that never heard the sound
Of thy loves pleading voice   15
Until his limbs were bound

5
Can God bring back the day when we two stood
Beneath the clinging trees in that dark wood

Notes

Line 4: A craze for ferns, or pteridomania (coined 1855 by Charles Kingsley) was prevalent in mid-nineteenth-century Britain. However, they were often used for decoration or as a design; Siddall's mention of them in their natural habitat is unusual. Ferns were extensively written about by botanists, many of them female; the ferns' aura of ancient worlds allies them to the craze for fossil-hunting, but they were also seen as magical, with the ability to render those who touched them invisible. As *The Language of Flowers* (London, 1834) suggests, they were also seen as representing love and sincerity.

Line 6: WMR's version reads "about thee flit".

Line 7: "the" is presumably "thee".

Line 8: See l.18 of "The Indian Serenade" by Percy Bysshe Shelley: "I die! I faint! I fail!"

Line 9: A line and a half is excised in the MS at the beginning of this stanza. It is nearly illegible but appears to read "Then I will [illegible] and my" and "Then will I [illegible]". Another illegible, deleted line appears before stanza 4.

Line 11: This seems to echo CGR's "A Better Resurrection", ll. 2-3: "My heart within me like a stone /Is numb'd too much for hopes or fears;" and l. 13: "My life is like a frozen thing,".

Line 12: Ll. 13-15 of CGR's "A Daughter of Eve": "stripp'd bare of hope and everything,/No more to laugh, no more to sing,/I sit alone with sorrow."

Line 13: The MS contains the deleted line "O frozen lips that uttered not a word". Lines 13-16 are not included in WMR's published version, and are evidently incomplete. They appear on the back of the MS for the rest of the poem.

Line 18: Another word, possibly "murky", is deleted and replaced with "clinging".

Line 18: See DGR's "A Portrait", which describes a painting of a woman in "A deep dim wood; and there she stands/ As in that wood that day:" (ll. 28-9). "A Portrait" is often read as a biographical counterpart to Siddall's "O silent wood".

The Ashmolean draft of "O silent wood" is monographed "EER"; the poem was first printed in the *Burlington Magazine*, May 1903 (pp. 291-2) along with WMR's memoir of his sister-in-law. The date of the poem is unknown, though Lasner suggests "summer 1857?" based on letters and poems (now lost) allegedly sent to DGR by his wife. The MS of this poem is in Siddall's handwriting, on a torn-out scrap of paper. Some illegible words (possibly an address) are scribbled on the bottom of the page.

The poem is frequently read biographically, perhaps in part due to Violet Hunt's comment that Rossetti had always made a habit of "lying about" in woods.[1] According to Hunt, who describes the wood in language clearly inspired by Siddall's poem, he also proposed to Siddall in a wood near Hastings:

> And there was the other wood, farther away, where she and Gabriel had gone so often to sit in the great dark hall of the over-arching trees, a light roof keeping off rain and the heat of the sun alike. She would lie flat under the low boughs, nearly down to the ground in some places, with waving fern fronds to fan her, and for long hours would watch the movements of the underworld, the tiny restrained gestures of the small things, shiny, furry, feathered: creeping, pottering and flying low among and under the different kinds of darknesses, mossy, velvety and dun like the shadows and corners of the human body. Low-leafed boughs of the larch, like eyelashes, stirred now and then by the grey flash of a bird.[2]

The liminal space of a wood, perhaps haunted or enchanted, is a common literary setting, however; this wood might recall the forest of Broceliande, where Merlin is spell-bound, trapped as though dead in an oak tree by Vivian, as recounted in Tennyson's "Merlin and Vivian" in *Idylls of the King* (1859). This is particularly relevant for the last quatrain.

The consistent and heavy rhythm and rhyme of the poem add to the monochrome picture, though the rhythm is frequently disrupted, grabbing the reader's attention. The poem is usually printed as a sonnet with the fourth stanza omitted, as WMR published it originally. Omitting the fourth stanza creates a sonnet (with rhyming couplets rather than the more common interlacing rhyme). The fourth verse and concluding couplet appear on the back of the paper with the rest of the

---

1   Violet Hunt, p. 111.
2   Violet Hunt, p.115.

poem. The 4-line stanzas are in iambic tetrameter, broadly, but with many substitutions; the fourth quatrain is less regular than the others and is probably incomplete.

The grey owl provides the only colour (however muted) in the poem, unlike many Pre-Raphaelite works. The description of the natural world is significant and detailed, however; the image of the clinging ferns and the voices of the trees suggest that the speaker is at one with nature, asking it to protect her ("ask of thee a boon"). Despite her unhappiness, she is not alone when surrounded by trees. Her misery is unspecific: as with many of CGR's poems, the source of sadness is absent, permitting the reader to associate more closely with the poem's emotions by putting themselves in the place of the speaker. CGR's poem "Repining", a poem which opens with waiting, echoing Tennyson's "The Lady of Shalott", also contains a reference to a "listening wood" to which "strange secrets" can be told (l. 216).

The poem may be related to Siddall's painting *The Haunted Wood* (1856, National Trust: Wightwick Manor). As Jan Marsh points out, this shows "a female figure meeting a ghost in woodland";[3] WMR says merely "a spectral subject".[4] The apparition seems frightening and unwelcome, with the figure of the woman in a plain, medieval-style dress, recoiling. The spectre is almost angelic in appearance, however, and one might read the woman's stance as a gesture of appeal rather than terror. The trees frame the figures, echoing the lines of their bodies and partly concealing the ghost, who seems to emerge from the tree-trunks, capturing the sense of haunting apparent in the poem. The background of Siddall's gouache bears some resemblance to DGR's "How They Met Themselves" (c.1860-4, with earlier ink drawing of 1851). This work is also linked to his poem "The Portrait", in which a double appears in a looking-glass.

---

3 Marsh, *Elizabeth Siddal: Pre-Raphaelite artist,* p. 64.
4 WMR, *Burlington Magazine* 1903 (p. 277)

Oh never weep for love that is dead

Oh never weep for love that is dead
Since love is seldom true,
But changes his fashion from blue to red,
From brightest red to blue,
And love was born to an early death　　　　　　　　5
And is so seldom true.

Then harbour no smile on your bonny face
To win the deepest sigh
The fairest words on truest lips
Pass on and surely die,　　　　　　　　　　　　10
And you will stand alone my dear,
When wintry winds draw nigh

Sweet, never weep for what cannot be
For this God has not given,
If the merest dream of love were true
Then, sweet, we should be in Heaven　　　　　　15
And this is only earth my dear
Where true love is not given

Notes

Line 1: Jeremiah 22:10, "Weep ye not for the dead".
Line 4: The bright colours remind the reader of her Pre-Raphaelite
associations. As WMR wrote, "In colouring our taste was all for bright

hues – red, blue, yellow, etc.".[5] Apparently Ruskin favoured blue for Siddall, while Rossetti preferred red, according to Violet Hunt, who refers to "Ruskin who loved blue and Rossetti who loved red", adding in a footnote, "He was a Jacobite simply because the Hanoverians had taken not only the azure out of the Garter but the vermilion out of the Royal Standard."[6] Finally, as Dinah Roe points out, "the colour blue is associated with chastity and loyalty, while red commonly symbolizes passion".[7]

Line 5: "For" is excised and replaced with "And" at the beginning of the line.

Line 7: Ashmolean fair copy has "bonny mouth", with "mouth" excised and replaced with "face". Published versions sometimes have "loving face".

Line 10: Fair copy has "Pass off".

Lines 15-18: Like both CGR and DGR, Siddall compares sacred and profane love here, constructing earthly love as barely a shadow of heavenly love. For DGR, this trope is perhaps most clearly seen in the sonnet sequence "The House of Life" and the accompanying paintings "Sibylla Palmifera" and "Lady Lilith". In CGRs work this approach is evident in many poems, including "The Convent Threshold", "A Triad" and "Monna Innominata". For CGR, the tension between *eros* and *agape* can only be resolved by renunciation of the earthly; in Siddall's poem, this leads to disappointment and cynicism.

The Bryson collection contains a fair copy by DGR and a draft by Siddall. The poem was first published in *RRP* (pp. 151-2). This is one of several poems which appear to have obvious links to Siddall's life, whether real or imagined. To scour her poems for biographical clues, however, does not tell us anything useful about the poems themselves. It may or may not relate to her relationship, but what we can know is that it is in a very regular poetic form, of iambic tetrameters and trimeters, for example. The occasional substitution, such as can be seen in the first

5 William Michael Rossetti, (ed.), *Dante Gabriel Rossetti. His Family-Letters with a Memoir*, 2 vols (London: Ellis & Elvey, 1895), p. 43.

6 Violet Hunt, p. 86.

7 Dinah Roe (ed.), *The Pre-Raphaelites from Rossetti to Ruskin* (London: Penguin, 2010), p. 348.

two feet in the third line, causes the reader to slow down and forces an emphasis onto the word "changes". Similarly, "was born to" in the fifth line again trips the reader, creating a pause for reflection. This is significant; it is not difficult to produce very regular verse, and a poem with no substitutions or pauses would soon lose the reader's attention. It requires an ear for poetry to place these stumbling blocks at the right moment, and the word "changes" is a crucial one, linking the structure of the poem with its focus on mutability and love which is "seldom true".

The second stanza opens, "Then harbour no smile on your bonny face/To win the deepest sigh". "Harbour" is an unusual word choice here, disrupting the rhythm and suggesting an intentional deception, yet "the fairest words on truest lips", by contrast, implies good intentions which will come to nothing. Lines such as this may have been why CGR commented on the poem's "cool bitter sarcasm", though describing it as her favourite, in a letter to DGR, February 1865.[8] "Deepest", "fairest" and "truest" echo each other in their suggestion of strong feeling, and yet the simple line "Pass on and surely die" quietly dismisses this emotion. In the penultimate line it becomes clear that the speaker is addressing a lover, as "my dear", anticipating their eventual separation once love has gone.

The final stanza again begins with a trochaic inversion, emphasising "sweet", and the first four lines jump around in the metre, throwing the emphasis onto "God" in the second line and "dream" in the third. The effect is one of barely restrained emotion, beginning to break away from the formal structure of the first two stanzas. Yet the closing lines, "And this is only earth, my dear,/Where true love is not given" return to a more regular, calm beat, as though the disruption of earthly love can pass and leave one with the peace of Heaven.

Though the poem is simple, it is not trite; rather, it draws on the conventions of medieval lyrics and also ballads. Marsh writes of "simple-seeming lyrics dramatizing a mood or emotion",[9] and this is true; the simplicity is on the surface. The poems tend to conform to ballad structures of quatrains with alternating lines of tetrameter and trimeter. The simple language and often melancholy subject matter also suit

---

8 Cited in William Michael Rossetti, *Rossetti Papers 1862 – 1870* (New York: Charles Scribner, 1903), p. 76.
9   Marsh, Jan, *The Legend of Elizabeth Siddal*, p. 198

Siddall's writing.

Hassett discusses potential sources in detail, including the reading that it is known Siddall did, such as Keats and Tennyson, but particularly Walter Scott's *Minstrelsy of the Scottish Border*, a copy of which she owned. The language, form and tone of the ballads can be seen in "Dead Love", as in her other poems. It also has thematic links with several of CGR's poems, which frequently focus on the transience of earthly love and the need to focus on the love of God. Though Siddall is not thought to have been conventionally religious, her poems nonetheless manifest a conventional hope in a greater love than is available on earth. Carol Rumens suggests that the speaker is a mother advising her daughter not to trust "true love". Rumens also comments on the effects Siddall is able to create with her lexical range:

> Siddal deploys a minimalist vocabulary to produce subtle shifts of emphasis. The chiasmus of the reds and blues in lines three and four is echoed in "if … love were true" and "where true love is not given". "Love" is repeated five times (always as a noun) and "true" four times, with an added variation, "truest". In the first stanza, "true" is the rhyme-word twice, as is "given" in the last. We have "dead", "death" and "die": "weep" occurs twice, and "sweet" is used twice as an endearment. Superlatives heighten the emotion in the middle stanza: "deepest", "fairest", "truest". The superlative becomes a form of diminution as "merest" in the last stanza, and the effect is poignant (compare "seldom").[10]

WMR's published version (1899), based on the Ashmolean fair copy, contains altered punctuation as well as two amended words in the second stanza. These amendments seem to attempt to regularise the text and tidy it up; the effect is to deaden some of the beauty of the poem, however.

---

10 Carol Rumens, "Poem of the Week: Dead Love by Elizabeth Siddall", *Guardian* 14 September 2015

Ope not thy lips thou foolish one

1
Ope not thy lips thou foolish one
Nor turn to me thy face
The blasts of heaven shall strike thee down
ere I will give thee grace

2
Take thou thy shadow from my path,   5
Nor turn to me and pray
The wild wild winds thy dirge may sing
Ere I will bid thee stay

3
Lift thy false brow from the dust,
Nor wild thine hands entwine   10
among the golden summer leaves
To mock the gay sunshine

And turn away thy false dark eyes
Nor gaze into my face
great love I bore thee now great hate   15
Sits grimly in its place

All changes pass me like a dream
I neither sing nor pray
and thou art like the poisonous tree
that stole my life away   20

Notes

Only verses 1-3 are numbered in the MS.

Line 3: The dramatic phrase "blasts of heaven" is a not uncommon one, used by Wordsworth and Shelley as well as appearing in hymns and sensation novels.

Line 8: "give thee grace" is crossed out and "bid thee stay" inserted; the former is a repetition and presumably the poet realised her mistake.

Line 9: An excised line reads: "Lift up thy false brow from out".

Line 11: This stanza is omitted from many published versions, including Lasner, but it appears in the MS and in its first publication by WMR in *Some Reminiscences*. The "summer leaves" are also used as a cruel contrast with unhappiness in "It is not now a longing year".

Line 13: Some published versions open this stanza with "Turn thou away"; in line 14, WMR substitutes "upon" for "into".

Line 19: This may be read as a reference to the fruit tree in the Garden of Eden. However, a significant influence here is likely to be William Blake's poem "A Poison Tree" (1794), in which the hatred felt by the speaker poisons all around him ("I was angry with my foe:/I told it not, my wrath did grow." (ll. 3-4).

A second MS draft in the Bryson bequest reads slightly differently:

Ope not thy lips thou foolish one
Look not to me thy face
the blasts of Heaven
shall strike thee down
Ere I will give this grace   5

Take thou thy shadow from my path
Nor turn to me and pray
the winds of Heaven may
sing thy dirge ere I will
bid thee stay   10

Lift thou thy brow from out the dust
nor wild thy hands entwine
among the golden summer leaves
to mock the gay sunshine

Turn thou away thy false dark eyes   15
nor gaze upon my face
Great love I bore thee
Now great hate sits grimly in its place

All changes pass me like a dream
I neither sing nor pray   20
and thou art like the poisonous
tree which stole my life away

Lasner suggests the poem may have been written in the Spring of 1857.[1] This MS is relatively clear to read, with few deleted words. Only verses 1-3 are numbered, however. The poem was first published in SR by WMR. In some subsequent reprintings, the third stanza is omitted. An illegible mark appears beside this stanza in the MS, which might indicate an intention to omit it, though whether the mark was made by Siddall or subsequent readers cannot be verified. The poem was heavily punctuated by WMR; what punctuation remains here is Siddall's own.

The phrasing and rhythm of this poem recall CGR's Maturin poems, particularly those inspired by *Women* (1818). WMR, editing these poems for publication after CGR's death, felt compelled to add that the poems must have originated in Maturin's novels, for otherwise "I should have been embarrassed to guess what directed my sister's pen to so singular a subject and treatment".[2] In particular, "Zara (Now the pain beginneth)" (1847) explores the strong emotions of love, hate, fear and jealousy, referring repeatedly to the falseness of the lover she chastises. This poem,

1 Lasner, p. 22.
2 *The Poetical Works of Christina Georgina Rossetti*, ed. William Michael Rossetti (London: Macmillan, 1904), p. 480.

which is also written in quatrains, refers to "burning love and hate" (l. 8) and asks,

> Hath the Heaven no thunder wherewith to denounce him?
> Hath the Heaven no lightning wherewith to chastise? (ll. 29-30)

The phrasing is strikingly different, but the concept of divine vengeance is aligned with that of lines 3-4 of Siddall's poem.

This poem is easily read as a demonstration of the complex relationship between Siddall and DGR, indicating the fluctuations in their affections which led them to put off marriage for so long. However, it would be equally valid to speculate whether, like her sister-in-law, Siddall might also be inspired by some fictional work in writing this poem.

David Latham describes the poem as "another feminist parody of two patriarchal traditions: courtly love rhetoric and in particular the cruel mistress lyric".[3] This indicates a poetic inspiration beyond the personal. Moreover, Hassett points out the central paradox of the poem:

> the cunning phrase "I neither sing nor pray." A denial that is literally impossible in a poem, this pseudo-statement plays upon the difference between a speaker disinclined to use words and the artist who makes a poem out of rhymed ballad stanzas.[4]

This suggests that, like CGR, Siddall uses women's silence (or potential silence) as a deliberate withholding that underlines their agency and ability to resist attempts to shape them.

---

3 Laurence W. Mazzeno, ed., *Twenty-first Century Perspectives on Victorian Literature* (Plymouth: Rowman & Littlefield, 2014), p. 141.
4 Hassett, p. 447.

Ruthless hands have torn her

1
Ruthless hands have torn her
from one that loved her well
Angels have up born her
Christ her grief to tell.

2
She shall stand to listen   5
She shall stand and sing
Till three winged angels
Her lovers soul shall bring.

3
He and she and the angels three
before God face shall stand   10
There they shall pray among themselves
and sing at His right hand.

Notes
Line 1: "Ruthless hands" is an obscure opening phrase, implying sudden, untimely death for which someone is at fault (rather than death in childbirth or through illness). It is a phrase often associated with murderers and madmen in nineteenth-century sensation fiction.
Line 9: An excised previous line reads: "Then he and she and the angels".
Line 9: The concluding image of "angels three" recalls Revelation 14: 6-12, in which three angels call the people on earth to repent and worship.

This poem was printed in *SR* II (p. 197), with the title "He and She and Angels Three". The poem above is taken from the Ashmolean MS draft in Siddall's handwriting (Bryson WA1977.182.6). At the top of the MS page is a fragment, which begins "Autumnal leaves are falling". There is a number 4 at the end, indicating the intention for a fourth stanza which was not written, or is lost. WMR made no changes to this poem for his publication, except for adding heavy punctuation and changing "up born" to "upborne".

The poem follows the familiar format of Siddall's oeuvre, with four-line stanzas of alternating lengths. The rhyme scheme is neat and does not deviate; however, the poem is saved from excessive tidiness by deviations from the rhythm which cause the reader to pause, such as the longer line "He and she and the angels three", which with its internal rhyme of repeated vowel sounds, emphasised by the archaic inversion of the last two words, adds a movement and softness to the stanza.

The poem indicates a conventional nineteenth-century interpretation of scripture which permits a reunion of loved ones in heaven, after the early death of a woman. The circumstances are obscure, perhaps in order for the poem to be applicable to the many circumstances which might cause the death of young women of the period (such as consumption or childbirth) and thus to bring Christian comfort to the bereaved. The poem offers a vague but universally appropriate consolation through the reminder of ultimate joy and reunion in Heaven, depicting a journey from tragic death to eternal joy.

Thy strong arms are around me love

1
Thy strong arms are around me love
My hand is on thy breast
Low words of comfort come from thee
Yet my soul is not at rest

2
For I am but a scared thing   5
Nor can I ever be
Aught but a bird whose broken wings
Must fly away from thee

3
I cannot give to thee the love
I gave so long ago   10
The love that turned and struck me down
Among the blinding snow

4
I can but give a tired heart
And weary eyes of pain
A faded mouth that cannot smile   15
And may not laugh again.

5
Yet keep thy arms around me love
Until I fall to sleep

Then leave me saying no good bye
Least I might fall and weep   20

Notes

Lines 3-4: WMR's version reads "Though words of comfort come from thee/ My soul is not at rest:"
Line 5: WMR's version has "startled" instead of "scared"
Line 7: WMR's version reads "Aught save".
Line 12: WMR: "Amid the blinding snow." For once, the weather appears to accord with the speaker's emotional state; the "blinding" indicates the blindness which love had once caused.
Line 13: WMR: "sinking heart", though the WMR fair copy reads "failing heart".
Line 17: WMR's version: "thine arms".
Line 18: WMR: "drop to sleep"
Line 20: WMR's draft reads "Lest I may wake, and weep." The published version in *RRP* has "Lest I might fall and weep." Some published versions have "Lest I might wake, and weep", a line which is excised in Siddall's draft.

This poem was first printed in *RRP*, p. 156, with the title "Worn Out". The published version in WMR's work is largely, though not completely, the same as the fair copy in the Bryson MS, which is in WMR's hand. The Bryson collection also contains a draft monographed EER, from which the poem above is taken.

This poem is structured in a similar way to many of her other poems, in four line stanzas with alternating line lengths and an abcb rhyme scheme. In form it resembles her ballads; however, in its subject it seems a much more personal poem, with little narrative form and no explanation of the speaker's circumstance, which perhaps explains the prevalence of biographical assumptions concerning this poem. The draft printed above indicates a poem which may well be incomplete, though some emendations in the MS indicate Siddall's work on it, but the irregularities of rhyme and metre which WMR's fair copy and published version attempt to smooth suggest a confidence with form and a willingness to subvert the expected forms.

This subversion is apparent in the poem's approach to love. In some ways this is an anti-love poem: Lines 13-15 list the attributes most often commented on in love poems (heart, eyes, mouth) but undermine the classic tropes of love poetry to indicate a poem that is rejecting traditional love. DGR uses these traditional markers of beauty and desire repeatedly in his poetry; for example, in "The Stream's Secret":

> For then at last we spoke
> What eyes so oft had told to eyes
> Through that long-lingering silence whose half-sighs
> Alone the buried secret broke,
> Which with snatched hands and lips' reverberate stroke
> Then from the heart did rise.

The physical markers of love are repeated throughout DGR's poem, embodying the relationship in a way which Siddall's approach seems to undermine. The same is true of "Life-in-Love" in *The House of Life*, which begins:

> Not in thy body is thy life at all
> But in this lady's lips and hands and eyes;
> Through these she yields thee life that vivifies
> What else were sorrow's servant and death's thrall.

For Siddall's speaker, love can no longer reside in the eyes, the mouth and the heart; they have been exhausted by the demands that love has placed upon them. The (presumably female) speaker is figured as the weaker party in the relationship, but the common trope of the Victorian woman as a caged bird is here subverted by images of the bird whose injury does not prevent them flying free. A desire to leave or be left indicates weariness not only with the lover but with love itself. Stefania Arcara writes of this poem:

> This brief dramatic monologue conveys a sense of exhaustion, tiredness, sleepiness, with literal and metaphorical meanings reinforcing each other: in the opening verses the female speaker, on the point of falling asleep in the arms of her lover, describes herself with vivid details, looking for comfort in the masculine embrace, but her emotional detachment from him is revealed in the stanza's concluding line.[5]

5 Arcara, p. 114.

To touch the glove upon her tender hand

1
To touch the glove upon her tender hand
To watch the jewel sparkle in her ring
Lifted my heart into a sudden song
As when the wild birds sing.

2
To touch her shadow on the sunny grass   5
To break her pathway through the darkened wood
Filled all my life with trembling and tears
And silence where I stood

3
To watch the shadows gather round my heart
To live to know that she is gone –   10
Gone gone for ever like the tender Dove
That left the Ark alone.

Notes

Line 7: The relationship and grief described here match that of Dante's
Vita Nuova, which DGR translated. "Trembling" is a word frequently
used by Dante, who is concerned that his tremors will betray his emotion
to others.
Line 9: WMR's version has "I watched".
Lines 9-10: A deleted line appears in the MS, which appears to read "To
know that she is gone".
Line 10: WMR's version has "To live".
Lines 11-12: The dove refers to the bird sent out from the ark to look

for dry land in Genesis; once dry land was found, it did not return. The dove is also used as a term of affection in the Bible, particularly in Song of Solomon, and Siddall was referred to as a dove by DGR (notably as a "meek unconscious dove" in a letter to CGR, 4th August 1852, and as "dear dove divine" in his poem "Valentine – To Lizzie Siddal"). A dove appears in *Beata Beatrix* (1864-70, Tate), DGR's most famous representation of Siddall as Dante's Beatrice, where it is taken to represent not love but death.

This poem first appeared in *RRP*, p. 153, under the title "Gone". Subsequently it was reproduced in *Emporium* along with an appreciative article on Siddall's work.[6] The Ashmolean MS (Bryson WA1977.182.6), on black-edged paper, is monogrammed EER. A fair copy by DGR is also in the Bryson collection.

Lasner points out that "This poem reminded CGR of Thomas Hood 'at his highest'",[7] and as Hassett suggests, poems such as Hood's "The Deathbed" would have been familiar to the Rossettis and perhaps Siddall, though less so to modern readers.[8] It is easy to see how, with its repeated words and simple form full of emotion, this echo of Hood might be the case.

There is also a medieval approach in the poem, in the distance between the couple so that it is her glove, her jewelled ring, and her shadow which have connected them, rather than any more physical contact. As the notes above suggest, there are also connections with Dante to be traced here. Both happiness and unhappiness are allied to nature in this and many other of her poems; in the "wild bird song" and the "trembling" in the wood, the poet plays with the illusion that the natural world echoes the speaker's emotional state. Hassett comments on the poem's "concluding reliance on the unreturning dove of Genesis 8:12 as a type of immortality".[9] As she notes, "the rhythmic slowing caused by the shortened last line would have registered with Christina whose preference

6   Zaira Vitale, "Eleonor Siddal Rossetti", *Emporium* 19 (1904), 430–47 (p.437).
7   Lasner, p. 23.
8   Hassett, p. 460.
9   Hassett, p. 460.

for a final, isolated trimeter is something of a prosodic hallmark".[10]

A potential source of inspiration for this poem might have been the *Vita Nuova*, where Dante writes of the joy he feels at even the most distant contact with Beatrice, and of his grief after her death. DGR translated the *Vita Nuova,* starting in the 1840s, and Siddall would certainly have known of his work; the Rossetti family all engaged with Dante and found it an inspiration for their own art and poetry in different ways. The trajectory of joy, trembling and grief follows that of Dante's poem. The poem bears witness to the male gaze, not unlike "I care not for my Ladys soul", since it "similarly exposes the artificiality of the male speaker's courtly posturing", while "[t]he Biblical allusion concluding the third and final quatrain ironically undercuts the exaggerated self-indulgence of the speaker".[11]

10 Hassett, p. 460.
11 Taylor, p. 37.

True Love

Farewell Earl Richard,
Tender and brave:
Kneeling I kiss
The dust from your grave.

Pray for me Richard,   5
Lying alone
With hands pleading earnestly,
All in white stone

Soon must I leave thee,
This sweet summer tide,
That other is waiting,   10
To claim his pale Bride.

Soon I'll return to thee,
Hopeful and brave,
When the dead leaves,
Blow over thy grave,   15

Then shall they find me
Close at thy head
Watching or waking,
Sleeping or dead.   20

Notes

Line 1: An "Earl Richard" also appears in Scott's *Minstrelsy*, in an eponymous ballad, though there he is not killed in battle but by a former mistress.

Line 4: Most published versions have "thy grave".

Line 10: "summer tide": Siddall's poems often contain references to summer as a time when bad things can happen, contrasting summer weather and green leaves, for example, with an inner sadness. The phrase also echoes many traditional ballads.

Line 11: This "other" bridegroom who will take her away is a common trope in ballads and also appears in CGR's poetry, such as "The Hour and the Ghost". In "True Love" one assumes the reference to the "other" is a living suitor, however, but the poem figures the dead as living and vice versa.

Line 20: Published versions have "fainting" instead of "waking", which appears in DGR's transcript of the poem.

This poem is the only one to which Siddall herself gave a title. The Bryson bequest contains two fair copies, one signed by EER and one by DGR. The poem was first printed in *RRP*, pp. 150-1.

The poem is loosely constructed as a ballad, with four-line stanzas containing lines of alternating length. The deviations from metre keep the reader's interest; they are cleverly done, so that the differing line lengths, some longer and some shorter, cause a hesitation and pause, intentionally impeding reading to slow down the casual reader.

The content is also that of a traditional ballad: a woman mourns at the tomb of her dead lover, who is constructed as a medieval knight, memorialised in marble. The faithfulness of woman to the end of life is here extolled, even beyond death. The poem resists over-archaic language, "summer tide" and "thy" being the only pseudo-medieval language used, but the image conveyed recalls Siddall's paintings "Before the Battle" (1858, Tate Gallery) and "The Woeful Victory" (?1848, Mark Samuels Lasner Collection), depicting a woman with a knight about to go into battle, and, in the second work, the corpse of the knight on the floor. The paintings take an explicitly medieval theme, and may all have been inspired by Scott and other contemporary ballads. As with many of her poems (and others of the time), the framework is an essentially Christian one in which reunion in Heaven is taken for granted; life, for the speaker, is something to be borne with patient suffering, united with an "other", until death reunites her with "Earl Richard".

Despite the critical tendency to read this poem as Siddall's personal reaction to the early death of Walter Deverell, who had introduced her to the Pre-Raphaelite Brotherhood (thus assuming she was in love with Deverell, as many biographers have done), the enthusiasm for medieval scenes she displays in her painting indicates the likely literary-historical source of this poem. Another potential source, both for this poem and perhaps the paintings mentioned, is the poem "The Bridal" by Emmeline Stuart-Wortley, published in *The Knight and the Enchantress* (1835). Here, too, there is a "pale Bride", who sees the death of her husband at the hand of a knight who attends their wedding-feast, and is proved to be the erstwhile lover of the bride, who had given him up for dead. She, too, kills herself in a fit of remorse and grief at the death of both previous and present lover: fidelity, of a kind, is hers in the end, but Siddall's poem indicates a more straightforward loyalty and love.

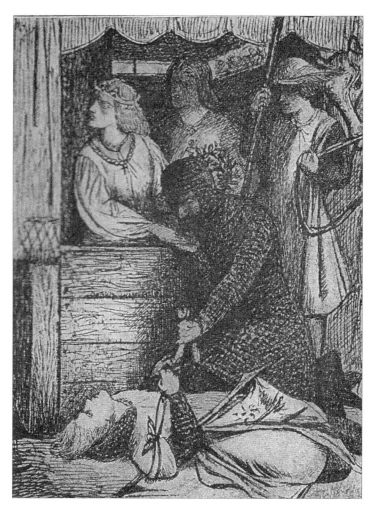

Image 5: Elizabeth Siddall, 1829-1862, "The Woeful Victory",
pencil, brown and black ink on paper, [1860]

Fragments

A golden flash of
sunlight woke him
down of the
leaves were still
they cause no ?   5
look a [two illegible words]
I came and this [two illegible words]

The wood was
flooded black and
heavy like a solid[?]   10
boding a [two illegible words]
Then the flowers keep
dropping to the [illegible word]
[illegible word] and Birds
[three illegible words]   15

Notes

Line 3: "the" is excised after "down".

This fragment is written with a leaking pen, and the additional
ink blots further obscure the words. It appears to describe a sleeper in
a wood, woken by the "golden flash of sunlight", perhaps intended to
accompany the fragment which begins "The sun was setting". Siddall's
fondness for woods as a setting for her poems and as a site of memory and
grief is apparent here, and the flowers dropping provides a parallel for the
speaker's anxiety, indicated in the "black and heavy" floods.

Knows a wood –
And bears its sleep
and dreams?
So is the memory of a love
where good was never found   5
Till waking by a unknown
stream
The angels gather round

Notes

Lines 4-5: These lines echo both the sentiment and the rhythm of "O never weep for love that's dead".

This torn-off fragment seems to echo "Ruthless hands have torn her" with its concluding line "The angels you then stand", and is probably an early draft for a stanza of this poem.

I am waiting for
the[e] by the swollen
brook yet I may meet
thee never with a
lovers look   5

Other eyes are gaze
ing into those deep eyes
of them yet they may
never answer the
loving[?] look on earth.   10

Oh Lord of Heaven
how is it that we may
have Hands true
hearts that wildly love
as upon this known Below   15
All is alone far above
But we were ever

Notes

Line 2: "the" is presumably intended to be "thee".

This fragment is in many ways more coherent than others collected here; the phrasing seems more developed, for example "I may meet/ thee never with a/lovers look", and "hearts that wildly love". There is the beginning of a rhyme scheme, so it is possible to see this as a draft for a poem never completed. The speaker regrets a love which is doomed, a topic many of Siddall's poems explore, and turn to conventional rhetorical questioning of God and a desire that all may become clear after death.

My goodbyes go
the grounds sink,
the dreary sun the day,
sees my woe
Oh Love thou   5
carry my shame
how wondrous [two illegible words]
That thought[?] look
forth and [illegible word] see rain
where thy dark   10
cares has been
Life thou art fading
from the will the
way before me I
shall I wake again   15
But once as when
my dreary eyes see
the light

Notes

Line 3: The "dreary sun" suggests that earthly light no longer holds any appeal for the speaker, a trope repeated in other poems by Siddall.
Line 5: The "Love" who is invoked to carry (presumably her burdens) echoes the lines in "Many a mile over land and sea":

And he came ready to take and bear
The cross I had carried for many a year (5-6).

It is possible that this is an early fragment which relates to later poems. Like "Life and night are falling from me", these lines suggest a sense of life coming to an end, and a desire to find peace after death. The images of light and darkness are familiar from her other poems, being traditional tropes of Christian salvation after the dark night of life, and this fragment concludes hopefully that the speaker's eyes will again see the light.

Now I see you dying
Now I see you flying
faces through the mist

day dreams sad and holy
Coming to me only   5
Through the mist of years

Shadows of the green fields
Shadows of the trees
Shadows of the tall stem[?] flowers
Shaking in the breeze   10

Shadows of the [two illegible words]
Shadows of the whole
Shadows of the [two illegible words]
Shading all my tears

Notes

This is clearly a fragment of a draft, some of which is illegible. Another
fragment appears in the Bryson collection which reads:

Now I see you dying
                flying
Faces through the mist

Day dreams sad or holy
Coming to me only
Through the weight of grief
Shadows of the green fields
                trees

None of this poem has been published before, given its fragmented state and partial illegibility, but it is possible to trace the poet at work here; both versions indicate working processes which consider the effect of repeated words. The imagery, of "faces through the mist" and of shadows, indicates a concern with past, lost loves which can be traced in Siddall's other poems, and is consistent with her naïve, medieval aesthetic. The first two stanzas recall a Dantesque vision of the dead just out of reach, appearing to a speaker in a trance-like state, while the subsequent stanza conjures the natural world as both a comfort and a barrier to reaching those in her dreams. The concept that the living are shadowed by the dead and visited by ghosts for whom they long is one which appears repeatedly in CGR's poetry, and the possibility of such a visitation in a day-dream is a common trope. Tennyson's long poem "The Day-Dream" likens a state of abstracted dreaming to the composition of poetry. Perhaps more significant is DGR's poem and picture "The Day-Dream"; the poem was not written until after Siddall's death, in 1880, while the picture was slightly earlier and based on a drawing of Jane Morris. Of course, as the *Rossetti Archive* points out, there is a "similar reverie depicted in *Beata Beatrix*".[12]

---

12   "The Day-Dream (for a Picture)", *The Complete Writings and Pictures of Dante Gabriel Rossetti*, edited by Jerome J. McGann, http://www.rossettiarchive. org/docs/7-1880.s259.raw.html [accessed 27.07.17].

The sun is setting
and the shafts of
harps were fading
Merry me o Birds
the air is filling   5
with the sound of
[illegible two words]

Land where they lived
Life is done shall
I see the starry   10
sun floods through
me the space of
heaven will all
these answers truly
no longer lie [illegible word]   15

Notes

An additional scrawled line down the side of the page reads:
    ? mystery, But
    opens ??
Line 1: MS contains an excised word ("the sun ~~was~~ setting").
Line 5: "was" is excised and replaced with "is".
Line 10: MS contains an illegible excised word after "I".
Line 12: "the" is repeated in the MS.

It is difficult to provide much interpretation of this scrawled and
frequently illegible fragment. It seems to offer a sense of longing,
mourning for one lost who will be restored to the speaker after death.
As with many of Siddall's poems, it suggests a hope that heaven will
provide the answers to questions of pain and sorrow for which earth has
no comfort. The poem seems linked in tone and language to "Life and

night are falling from me", in which the desolateness of the world in the absence of a loved one is lamented along with a celestial vision of the air filling with angel sounds, providing hope for future heavenly solace.

APPENDIX A

Letter to Emma Madox Brown on the back of one draft of stanzas for "It is not now a longing year". The letter is undated, and is reproduced here as it is not available in print elsewhere. It appears to be a draft, containing various phrasings of the same request.

Dear Emma

If you are in town and have nothing better to do I should much like to see you as I am about to leave England.

I am about to leave England and so if you are in town I should much like to see and tell you one or two things before I go. If therefore you have nothing better to do, I will meet you by the park and library where the Buses stop as we could then walk into the park and have a chat

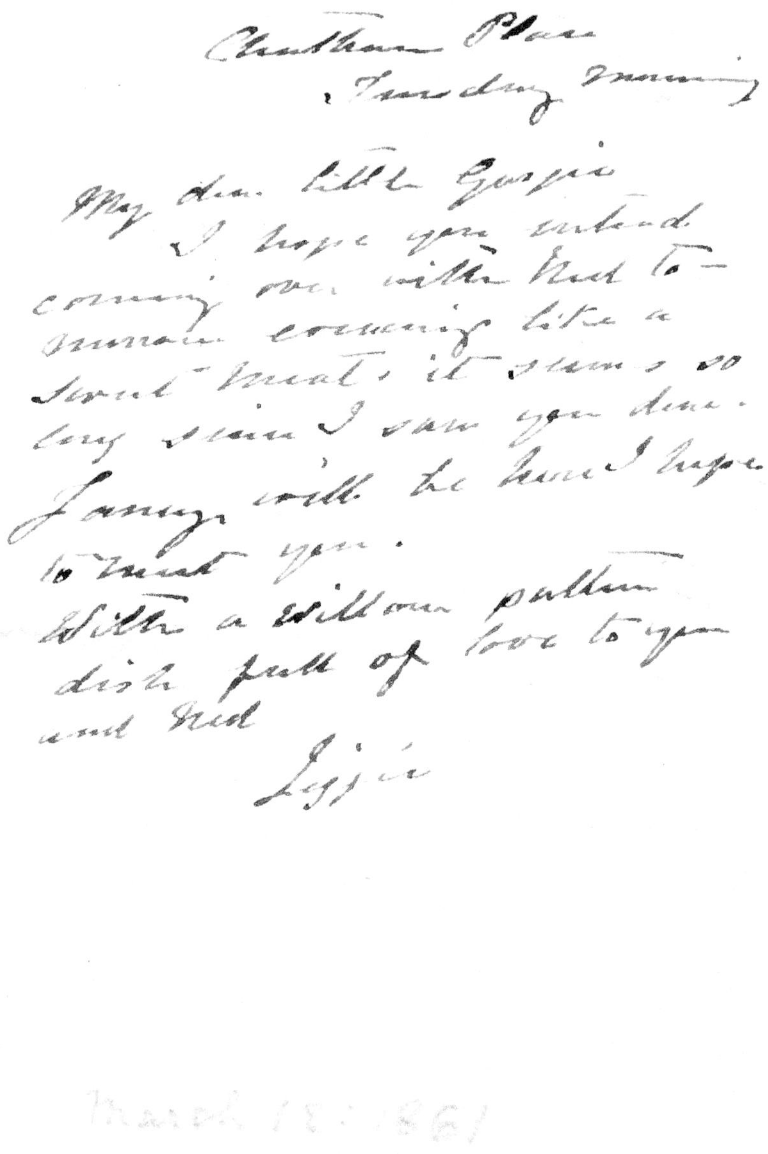
Chatham Place
Tuesday morning

My dear little Georgie
I hope you intend
coming over with Ned to-
morrow evening like a
sweet treat; it seems so
long since I saw you dear.
Janey will be here I hope
to meet you.
With a willow pattern
dish full of love to you
and Ned
Lizzie

March 12 1861

Image 6: Elizabeth Siddall, 1829-1862, Autograph letter signed to Georgiana Burne-Jones, 12 March 1861 (Mark Samuels Lasner Collection, on loan to the University of Delaware Library)

APPENDIX B

Poems frequently associated with Siddall and her own writing

Christina Rossetti, "In an Artist's Studio" (1856; pub. 1896)

One face looks out from all his canvases,
One selfsame figure sits or walks or leans:
We found her hidden just behind those screens,
That mirror gave back all her loveliness.
A queen in opal or in ruby dress,
A nameless girl in freshest summer-greens,
A saint, an angel — every canvas means
The same one meaning, neither more or less.
He feeds upon her face by day and night,
And she with true kind eyes looks back on him,
Fair as the moon and joyful as the light:
Not wan with waiting, not with sorrow dim;
Not as she is, but was when hope shone bright;
Not as she is, but as she fills his dream.

Dante Gabriel Rossetti, "The Portrait" (1847; pub. 1870)

This is her picture as she was:
It seems a thing to wonder on,
As though mine image in the glass
Should tarry when myself am gone.
I gaze until she seems to stir,—
Until mine eyes almost aver
That now, even now, the sweet lips part
To breathe the words of the sweet heart:—
And yet the earth is over her.

Alas! even such the thin-drawn ray
That makes the prison-depths more rude,—
The drip of water night and day
Giving a tongue to solitude.
Yet only this, of love's whole prize,
Remains; save what in mournful guise
Takes counsel with my soul alone,—
Save what is secret and unknown,
Below the earth, above the skies.

In painting her I shrin'd her face
Mid mystic trees, where light falls in
Hardly at all; a covert place
Where you might think to find a din
Of doubtful talk, and a live flame
Wandering, and many a shape whose name
Not itself knoweth, and old dew,
And your own footsteps meeting you,
And all things going as they came.

A deep dim wood; and there she stands
As in that wood that day: for so
Was the still movement of her hands
And such the pure line's gracious flow.
And passing fair the type must seem,
Unknown the presence and the dream.
'Tis she: though of herself, alas!
Less than her shadow on the grass
Or than her image in the stream.

That day we met there, I and she
One with the other all alone;
And we were blithe; yet memory
Saddens those hours, as when the moon
Looks upon daylight. And with her
I stoop'd to drink the spring-water,
Athirst where other waters sprang;

And where the echo is, she sang,—
My soul another echo there.

But when that hour my soul won strength
For words whose silence wastes and kills,
Dull raindrops smote us, and at length
Thunder'd the heat within the hills.
That eve I spoke those words again
Beside the pelted window-pane;
And there she hearken'd what I said,
With under-glances that survey'd
The empty pastures blind with rain.

Next day the memories of these things,
Like leaves through which a bird has flown,
Still vibrated with Love's warm wings;
Till I must make them all my own
And paint this picture. So, 'twixt ease
Of talk and sweet long silences,
She stood among the plants in bloom
At windows of a summer room,
To feign the shadow of the trees.

And as I wrought, while all above
And all around was fragrant air,
In the sick burthen of my love
It seem'd each sun-thrill'd blossom there
Beat like a heart among the leaves.
O heart that never beats nor heaves,
In that one darkness lying still,
What now to thee my love's great will
Or the fine web the sunshine weaves?

For now doth daylight disavow
Those days,—nought left to see or hear.
Only in solemn whispers now
At night-time these things reach mine ear;

When the leaf-shadows at a breath
Shrink in the road, and all the heath,
Forest and water, far and wide,
In limpid starlight glorified,
Lie like the mystery of death.

Last night at last I could have slept,
And yet delay'd my sleep till dawn,
Still wandering. Then it was I wept:
For unawares I came upon
Those glades where once she walk'd with me:
And as I stood there suddenly,
All wan with traversing the night,
Upon the desolate verge of light
Yearn'd loud the iron-bosom'd sea.

Even so, where Heaven holds breath and hears
The beating heart of Love's own breast,—
Where round the secret of all spheres
All angels lay their wings to rest,—
How shall my soul stand rapt and aw'd,
When, by the new birth borne abroad
Throughout the music of the suns,
It enters in her soul at once
And knows the silence there for God!

Here with her face doth memory sit
Meanwhile, and wait the day's decline,
Till other eyes shall look from it,
Eyes of the spirit's Palestine,
Even than the old gaze tenderer:
While hopes and aims long lost with her
Stand round her image side by side,
Like tombs of pilgrims that have died
About the Holy Sepulchre.

APPENDIX C

According to Violet Hunt, William Allingham wrote this poem for Siddall on the night he met her, full of premonitions of her unfortunate involvement with the Brotherhood and Rossetti. The poem is (mis)quoted in Hunt, p. 27.

The Cold Wedding

But three days gone
Her hand was won
By suitor finely skill'd to woo
And now come we
In pomp to see
The Church's ceremonials due.

The Bride in white
Is clad aright,
Within her carriage closely hid
No blush to veil
For too, too pale
The cheek beneath each downcast lid.

White favours rest
On every breast;
And yet methinks we seem not gay.
The church is cold,
The priest is old, —
But who will give the bride away?

Now delver, stand.
With spade in hand,
All mutely to discharge thy trust:
Priest's words sound forth;

They're – "Earth to earth,
"Ashes to ashes, dust to dust."

The groom is Death;
He has no breath;
(The wedding peals, how slow they swing!)
With icy grip
He soon will clip
Her finger with a wormy ring.

A match most fair,
This silent pair,
Now to each other given for ever,
Were lovers long,
Were plighted strong
In oaths and bonds that could not sever.

Ere she was born
That vow was sworn;
And we must lose into the ground
Her face we knew:
As thither you
And I, and all, are swiftly bound.

This Law of Laws
That still withdraws
Each mortal from all mortal ken –
If 'twere not here;
Or we saw clear
Instead of dim as now; – what then?
This were not Earth, and we not Men.

Printed in Great Britain
by Amazon

22999351R00066